# THE FOUR HEATONS

## THROUGH TIME

Heaton Moor, Heaton Mersey,
Heaton Chapel & Heaton Norris

Ian Littlechilds & Phil Page

AMBERLEY PUBLISHING

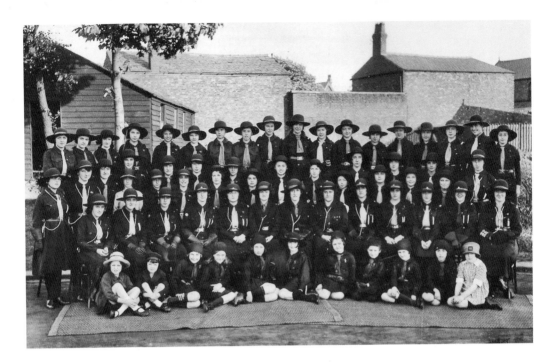

## Heaton Moor Girls Guides Group, 1917

The Heaton Moor Guides group outside their Guide hut on Kings Road in 1917. The girl on the far left of the third row from the front is Barbara Lobel (*née* Hobson), who lived in the Heatons from 1903 until her death in 1998. Some of her memories about life in the Heatons in the early part of the twentieth century are included as part of the Introduction.

## About the Authors

Ian Littlechilds and Phil Page are local freelance photographers who have been working together on a wide range of photographic projects since 2005. The idea for this book started with work produced for an exhibition of photographs and old postcards displayed in the Heatons Library in 2012. Although they have both been published in other fields, this is their first book that combines old and new photographs with an element of local history.

First published 2013

Amberley Publishing
The Hill, Stroud, Gloucestershire, GL5 4EP
www.amberley-books.com

Copyright © Ian Littlechilds & Phil Page, 2013

The right of Ian Littlechilds & Phil Page to be identified as the Authors of this work has been asserted in accordance with the Copyrights, Designs and Patents Act 1988.

ISBN  978 1 4456 2059 6 (print)
ISBN  978 1 4456 2066 4 (ebook)

British Library Cataloguing in Publication Data.
A catalogue record for this book is available from the British Library.

Typesetting by Amberley Publishing.
Printed in Great Britain.

# Introduction

The area occupied by the Four Heatons was originally fairly poor agricultural ground located between the north of Stockport and the southern edges of Manchester. The name 'Heaton' is derived from the Anglo-Saxon for a farming enclosure on a heath or high ground. The four areas we know today started to develop their own identities around the mid-1700s, when the building of St Thomas' church on Manchester Road, consecrated in 1765, resulted in the area becoming known as Heaton Chapel. Heaton Mersey was originally an area within the long-established Heaton Norris township, but developed its own identity with the coming of the bleaching, printing and brickmaking industries in the mid- to late 1800s. This industrialisation, and the coming of the railways, resulted in Heaton Moor, and other parts of the Heatons, becoming popular places to live. Many wealthy Victorians built their houses there, with spectacular views across to the Cheshire Plain, the Peak District, Alderley Edge or the Pennines.

Housing developments grew quickly through the interwar years. In the advertising material for new homes constructed by local builder W. H. Hammond, Heaton Mersey was described as 'a delightfully modern and high class residential area, free from anything suggestive of overcrowding, for those who desire bracing breezes and rural amenities in an attractive spot of inestimable value'. T. Costello, who built many of the houses around Heaton Moor Park, promised local buyers that 'there is a something about the district which is irresistible. It may be its assurance of charm, the freshness of the air, or its settled and peaceful look. Whatever it be suggests a new standard of home life. It confirms your sudden conviction that this is the place of your desire' (Green, Frank, *Manchester and District Old and New* [London Souvenir Magazines, 1935]).

Apart from the build-up of traffic and the pockets of modern development, the buildings, roads and layout of the Heatons have changed little since the first half of the twentieth century. Consequently, the area retains a strong visual connection with the past through its Victorian and Edwardian architecture, parks, churches and traditional public houses. These are the same streets and open spaces that Barbara Hobson would have frequented as a child, and it is worth exploring some of her memories to connect with what life would have been like in the Heatons a century ago.

The district I lived in was quiet; some people called it the 'Heaton Moor Village'. There were nine shops with a veranda over half of them at our end of the Moor. Early in the morning, the milk cart came round with two big churns filled with milk. We went out with our milk jugs and bought our milk straight from the milkman and, if we wished, got fresh cream to put on our porridge.

The bread van came each day with fresh bread and buns. On Tuesdays, the fishman called and would fillet the fish for you ready for cooking. Then we had a 'rag and bone' cart come round with balloons and windmills ready to give anyone who gave him old carpets or other unwanted goods.

Friday was the day that the muffin man called, selling hot muffins, 'pikelets' or oatcakes, which my father really liked.

In the old days, hansom cabs waited outside the railway station on Heaton Moor Road to convey passengers off the trains to the top end of the Moor. It was a lovely sound to hear the clatter of horses' hooves trotting over the cobbled road. I thought it a real treat to have a ride in a hansom cab to the top of the Moor at sixpence (in old money).

One day a 'German band', consisting of four men, came down the road with a dancing bear. It had a chain around its waist. I felt very sorry for the bear, it didn't look happy. It moved its feet up and down in time to the music that the men were playing on their instruments. I was frightened it would escape and chase me.

When the 1914–18 war was on I frequently used to climb on the fence by the railway track to watch the hospital trains pass and wave to the wounded soldiers. I was thrilled when I got a wave back from any of them.

Barbara lived in the Heatons for almost the whole of the twentieth century, first on Cedar Grove and then on Peel Moat Road. The Heatons have always been a place where people have stayed, and this undoubtedly accounts for the sense of community that has developed over the past 100 years – the reason why so many people settle in the area today.

# Acknowledgements

We would like to thank the following people and organisations for their help in compiling the old photographs of the Heatons and reminiscences that have been incorporated into the text: Margaret Myerscough and the staff at the Stockport Heritage Library; Phil Rowbotham and Mary Griffiths James from the Stockport Heritage Trust; the staff at the Heatons Public Library; Richard and Dan Wardle; Brian Lowe; David Broadhurst; Diane Connell; Joseph and Carolyn Canning for supplying the memoirs of Barbara Hobson; Sunnyfield Road residents, who turned out in force to complement the VE Day picture; Freddie and Jessie Dixon; Tom and Joy Gibbons; Marion Harris; Priestnall School pupils Martha Collins, William Renshaw and Rahul Arya; Renolds plc; English Heritage; Aerofilms Ltd; Boots plc.

We would like to thank all those listed above for the permission granted to reproduce the copyright material in this book. Every effort has been made to trace copyright holders and to obtain their permission for the use of copyright material.

We would also like to acknowledge the following publications, which were an invaluable source of information when researching some of the facts to go with the photographs: Jones, Elizabeth, *Old Heatonians* (Stockport Libraries, 1997); Heaton Mersey Research Group, *Heaton Mersey. A Victorian Village. 1851–1881* (Stockport Historical Society, 1985); Rowbotham, Phil, *Heritage Walk Series*, Editions 5, 6 and 9 (Stockport Heritage Trust).

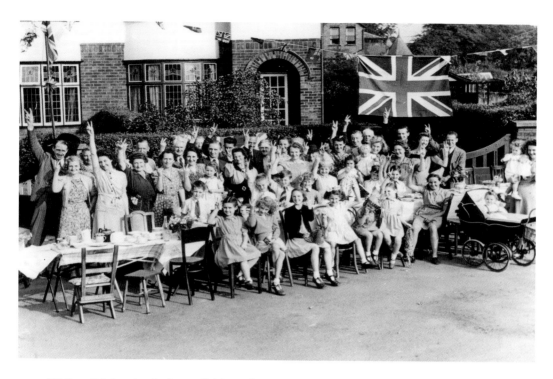

**VE Day Celebration in Sunnyfield Road, 1945 and 2013**
A street party took place to mark the end of the Second World War outside the Wardles' house, No. 21 Sunnyfield Road. The Wardles, Marshes, Lowes, Halls, Elders, Roberts, Gouldings, Maddocks, Powells, Bakers, Whittakers, Warnes, Royals, Derbyshires, Gadsburys, Garnetts and Adamsons were all there. Afterwards, an effigy of Hitler was burnt, damaging the road for a number of years hence. The residents of today were only too willing to pose for a photograph.

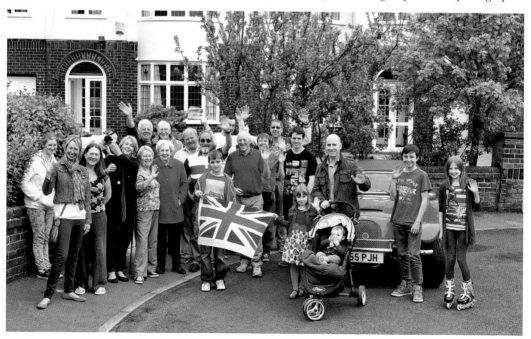

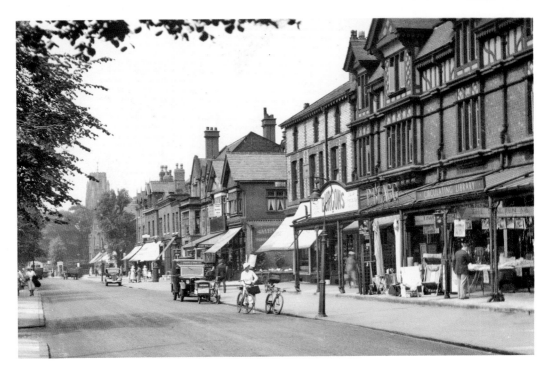

**Heaton Moor Road, 1937 and 1965**

The opening of Heaton Chapel station transformed the development of the area around Heaton Moor Road. The familiar row of shops was constructed with Victorian wrought-iron supports and glass canopy awnings, which are still a feature today. There have been few changes over the years, and there continues to be a good range of local shops, cafés and restaurants in the area.

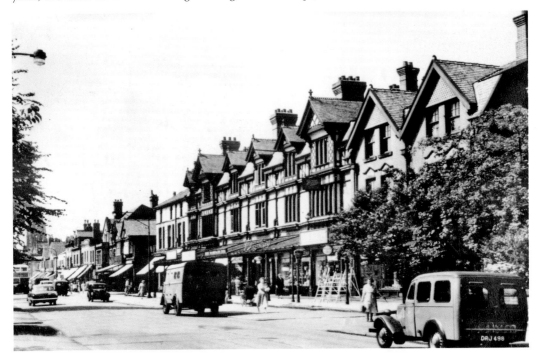

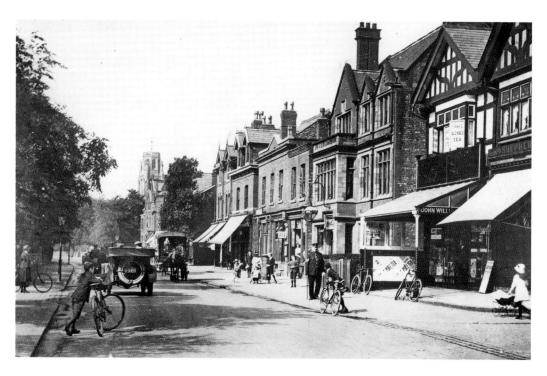

**Heaton Moor Road, 1923 and 2013**

Most of the shops have survived over the years, with the exception of those at the southern end, which were removed when the original buildings were demolished and replaced with a supermarket and hairdresser's. Part of the pavement has also been removed to accommodate the many vehicles that now use this busy road.

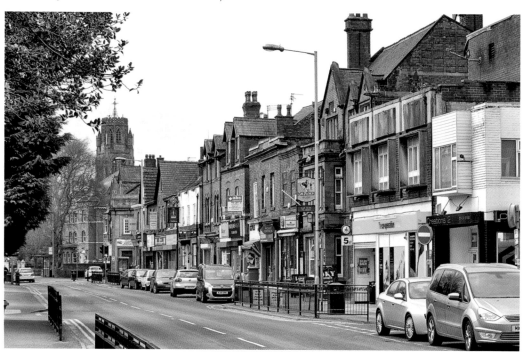

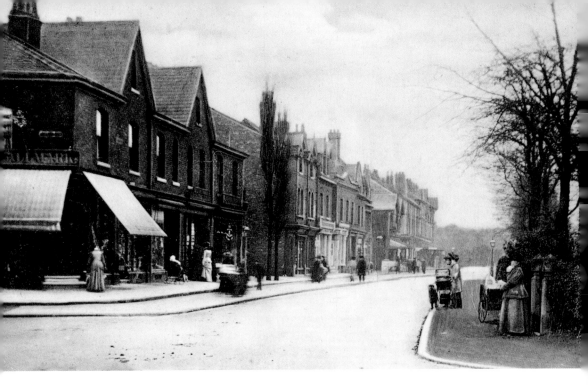

**Heaton Moor Shops, 1905 and 2013**

This view north, towards the station, shows the development of the shops providing for the residents of the affluent suburb, which was developing with the new commuter links to Manchester. The shop on the corner, originally George Hallmark's Bakers and Flour Dealers, has undergone a few changes over the years, but has recently been modernised to provide locals with the café-bar experience of Kro Bar.

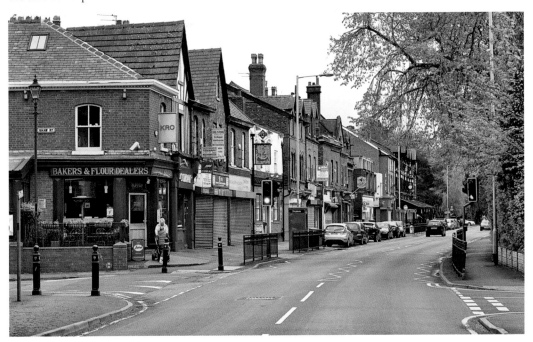

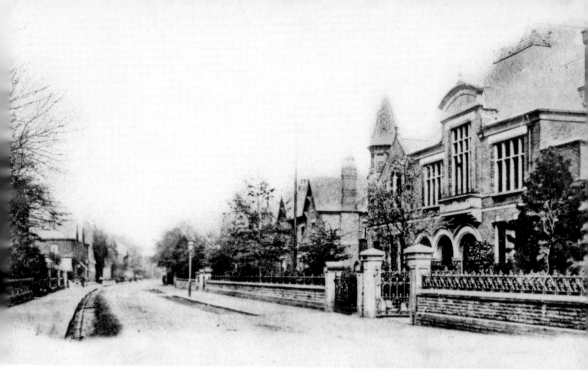

**The Reform Club, Heaton Moor, 1904 and 2013**
Intellectual life in Heaton Chapel was provided for when the Reform Club was built by architect Alfred Darbyshire in 1886. It was used to provide housing for 'Liberal gentlemen' and glamorous social events were held in the Reform Hall; the club was often visited by Lloyd George. Planning permission was granted in 2010 to convert the building into a number of modern apartments.

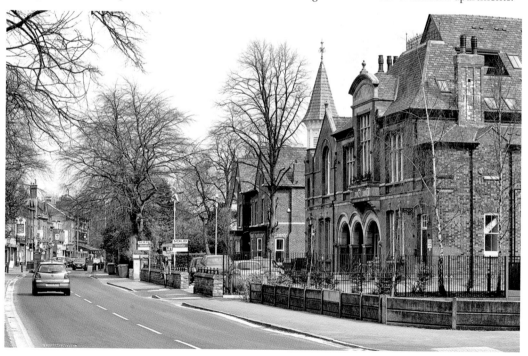

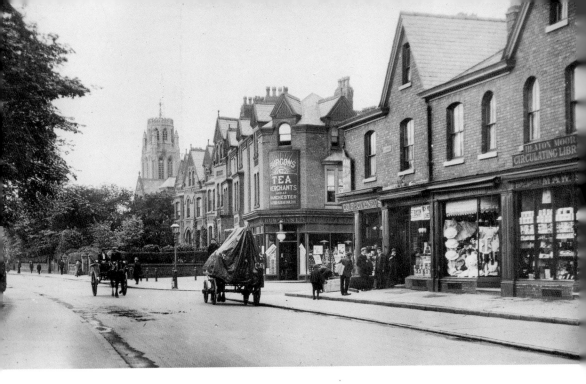

**The Corner of Shaw Road and Heaton Moor Road, 1908 and 1918**
The building on the corner of Shaw Road and Heaton Moor Road has served the area well over the years. In 1907 it housed Burgons Limited, a tea and coffee establishment, and by 1918 it had become Cliff and Brown's, a draper's and milliner's. A good hat was the mark of a gentleman, and men returning from the allied forces were obliged to wear a hat for a certain time as part of their demobilisation process.

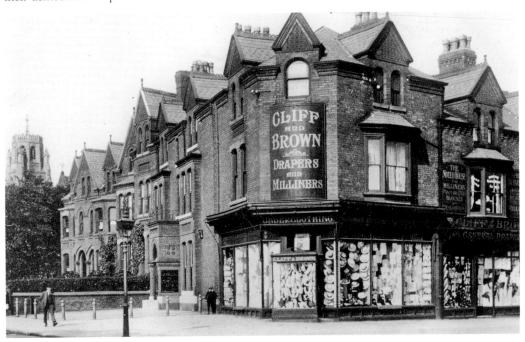

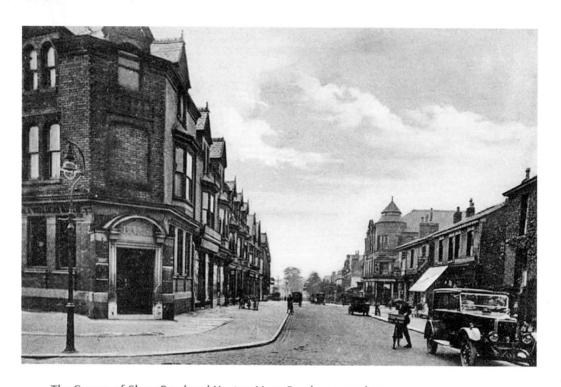

### The Corner of Shaw Road and Heaton Moor Road, 1935 and 2013

By 1935, the building had become a bank owned by Martins. The original entrance to the bank was at the side of the building on Heaton Moor Road, but the closure of the hat shop allowed the bank to occupy a larger area. It was eventually taken over by Barclays Bank, but later housed a firm of solicitors. At the time of publication, the building was vacant and up to let.

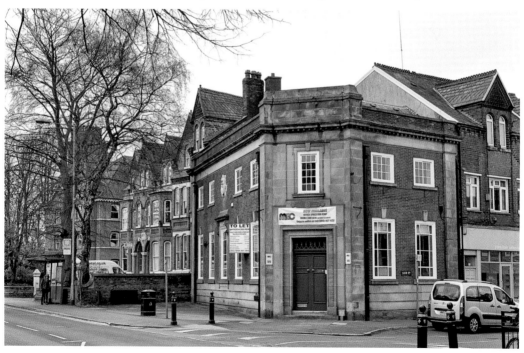

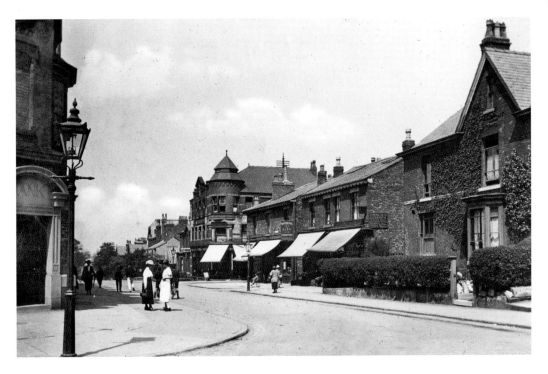

**Shaw Road, 1927 and 2013**

Shaw Road has always been a popular shopping area in the Heatons. The sign from George Hallmark's Bakery, proclaiming 'Bakers and Flour Dealers', has survived through numerous commercial changes to still be seen today. The shops complemented those on Heaton Moor Road and extended down into Derby Range where William Wray's 'Fried Fish and Chimney Sweep' premises could be found.

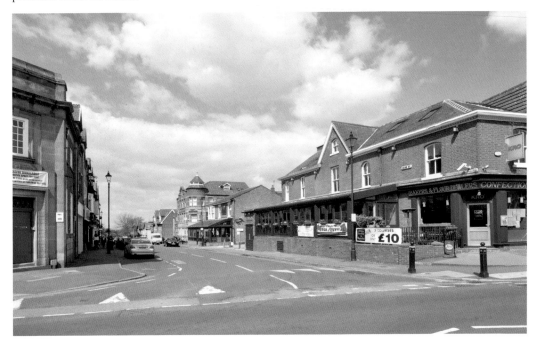

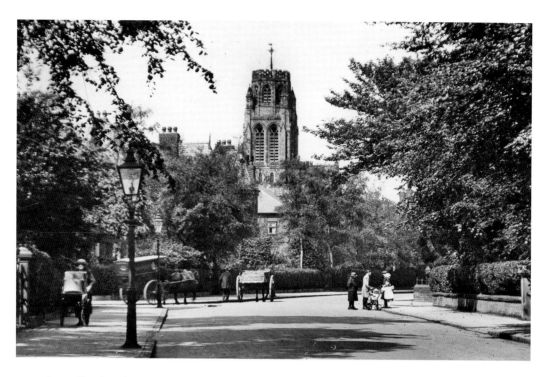

**St Paul's Church, Heaton Moor Road, 1920 and 2013**

St Paul's church was a dominant feature when travelling along Heaton Moor Road towards Wellington Road. The church was opened on Friday 29 September 1876 and was consecrated on Thursday 25 January 1877. The octagonal tower was completed in November 1900 at a cost of £1,980. The enlargement of the church was completed in 1896. This was required due to the increase in population in Heaton Chapel and Heaton Moor. The tree foliage now restricts the view of the church during spring and summer.

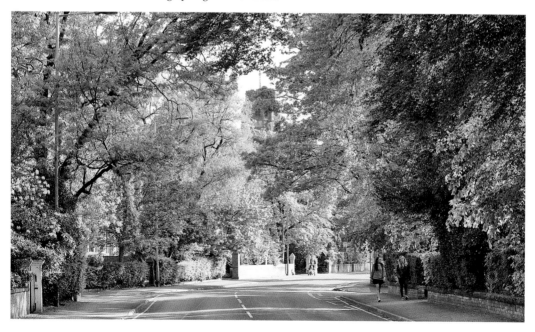

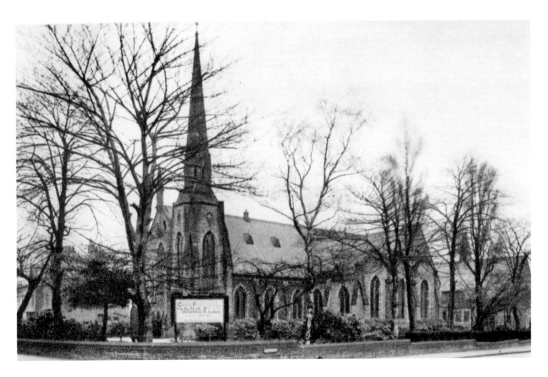

**Heaton Moor Methodist Church, 1920 and 2013**

Heaton Moor Methodist church was built in 1894, but was pulled down and rebuilt in the early 1980s. It was designed by local architects in a more modern style, incorporating the original stained-glass window and stone tracery. The window can be seen shining brightly on Heaton Moor Road each evening.

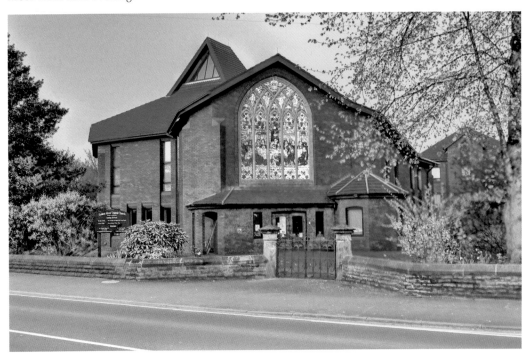

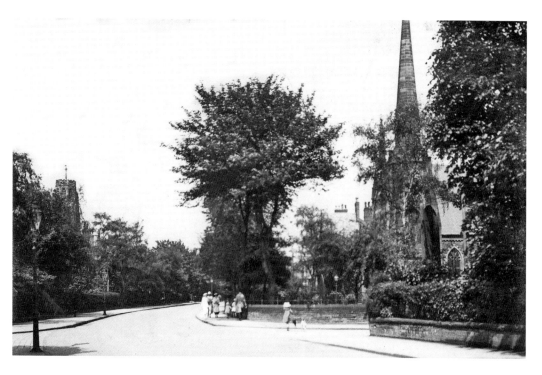

**Heaton Moor Road, 1920 and 2013**
The two churches, St Paul's on the left in the photograph, and Heaton Moor Methodist church on the right, can be seen clearly in the 1920 photograph. However, the trees have grown extremely well along Heaton Moor Road since 1852, from the time when Heaton Chapel station was built, and the area began to prosper. The Methodists now worship in partnership with the United Reformed Church.

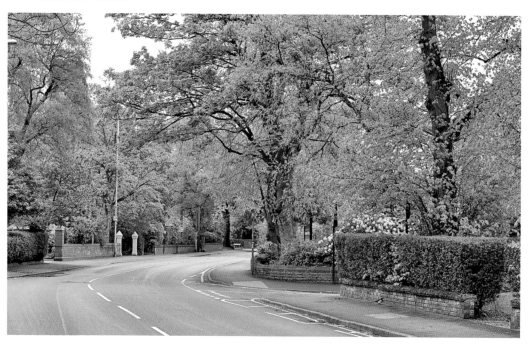

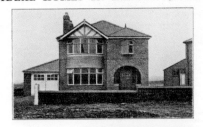
**Buckingham Road Development, 1930 and 2013**

The Heatons was subject to an extensive housebuilding programme in the 1930s, with groups of affordable housing appearing on rural land acquired by local builders such as T. Costello and W. H. Hammond. Typical of these developments were the houses along Buckingham Road and Peel Moat Road, and the sales literature proclaimed Heaton Moor as 'a wonderful district, combining with it all that gives health, enjoyment and happiness'.

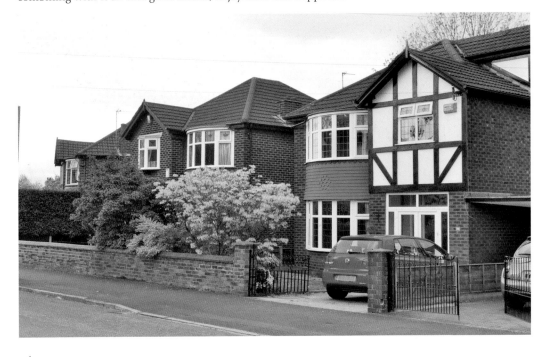

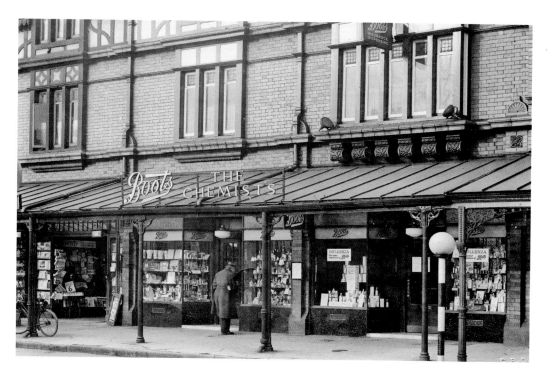

**Boots the Chemists, Heaton Moor Road, 1937 and 2013**

The pharmacy chain of Boots was founded in 1849 by John Boot. However, it was his son, Jesse, who had the ambition for the company to become a nationwide chain. An outlet on Heaton Moor Road has been here for well over seventy-five years. The shop window is displaying influenza products, possibly with the No. 7 and Soltan ranges, both of which were introduced during the 1930s. Today, the window dressing is advertising ways of saving time on trips to the surgery.

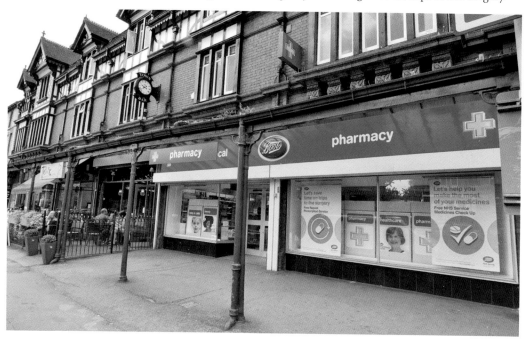

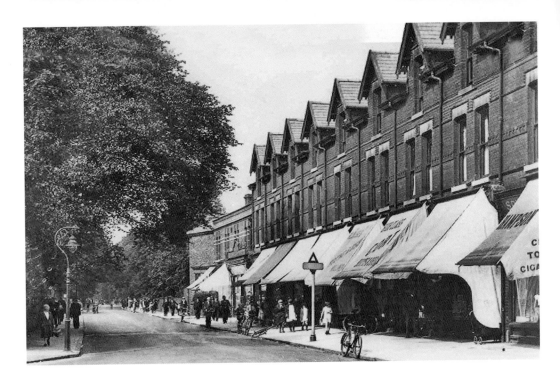

## Moor Top Shops, 1930s and 2013

This busy scene from the 1930s shows how the shops at Moor Top had developed and expanded to match the more established shops at the station end of Heaton Moor Road. Today the shops continue to offer a good variety of local shopping opportunities, and Juniper Café has added a touch of the pavement café experience for local shoppers.

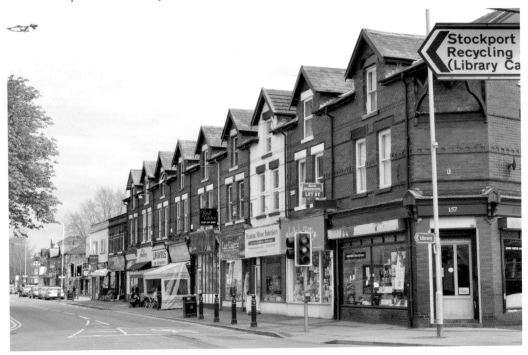

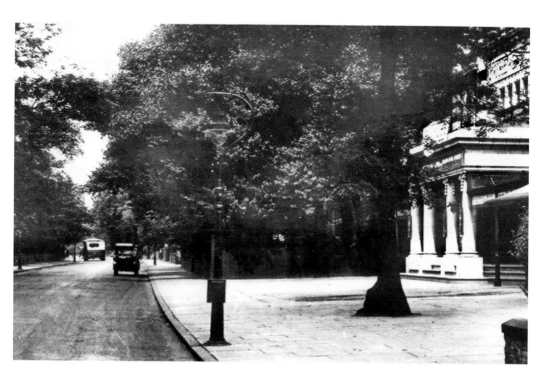

### The Savoy Cinema, 1930s and 2013

The Savoy was opened in 1923 and originally had stalls and a balcony with seating for over 1,000 people. The first film shown was a silent version of *The Virgin Queen* starring Diana Manners. In the early 1930s, the Savoy was adapted for 'talkies' but was badly damaged by fire in 1938. In the Second World War, it served as an evacuation centre for local families, and was eventually refurbished in 1971, when the impressive façade was boxed in to create a larger foyer area.

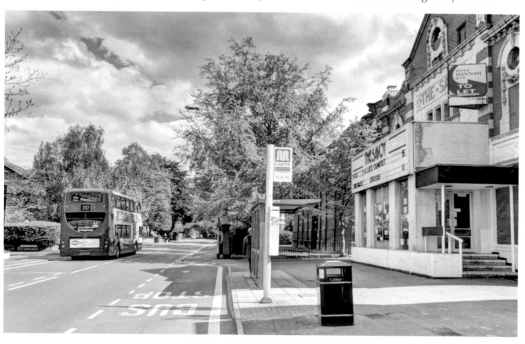

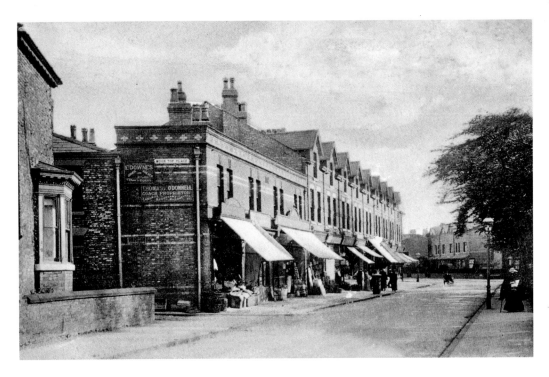

**Moor Top Shops, 1907 and 2013**

In 1884 there were only a few cottages in this area, known as Owler Nook. By 1872 the first shops had been built around the east side of Heaton Moor Road, and by 1915 the shops had extended into Moorside Road. They provided a good range of services for the local community, including a wine merchant, a bakery, a butcher, two greengrocers and Franklands stationery and newspaper shop.

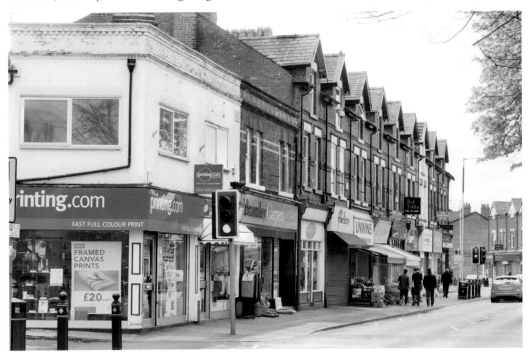

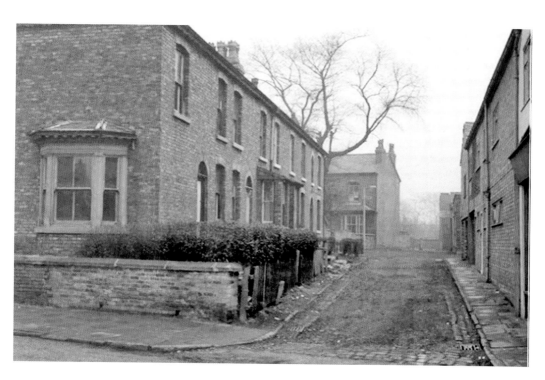

Hawthorn Terrace, 1972 and 2013

Hawthorn Terrace is a narrow street, running between the shops on Heaton Moor Road and the housing and land at the rear of Hawthorn Grove. This view from around 1970 shows the original terraced housing, which flanked some larger properties on Heaton Moor Road. These have since been demolished and replaced with a row of shops and flats, built in functional style.

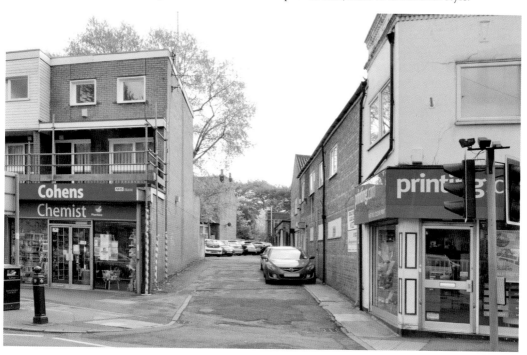

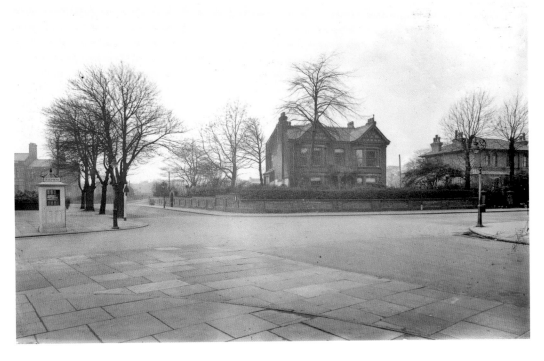

## Moor Top Centre, 1930s and 2013
In the 1930s, three large villas stood next to the Victorian building, which is now an estate agent. Berne Cot, Dunbar and Beech House were built around 1871. Berne Cot was built in colonial style by its owner, who was inspired by his service in the Bengal Lancers. Beech House has since been demolished to make way for a supermarket, but Bern Cot and Dunbar remain, albeit with redesigned ground floors to accommodate local businesses.

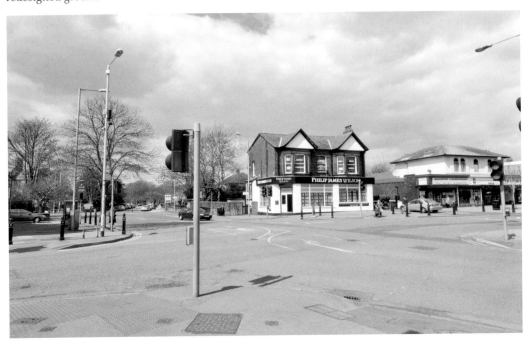

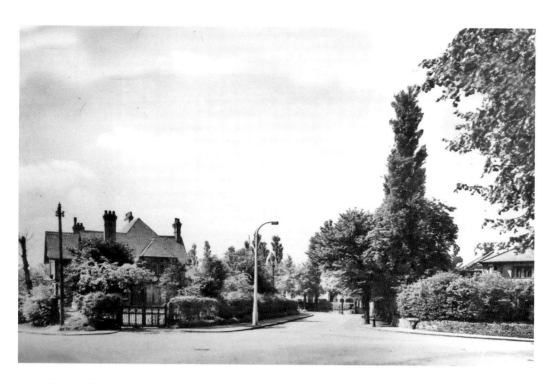

### Queens Drive Junction, 1930s and 2013

The intersection of Queens Drive, Thornfield Road and Bank Hall Road would have been a busy junction on the main route from Heaton Moor Road to Didsbury Road in the early part of the century. By the 1930s, however, Moorside Road had been opened to provide a more direct route for traffic, resulting in an altogether more tranquil setting. The large Victorian house on the left has been demolished and replaced with a modern flats complex.

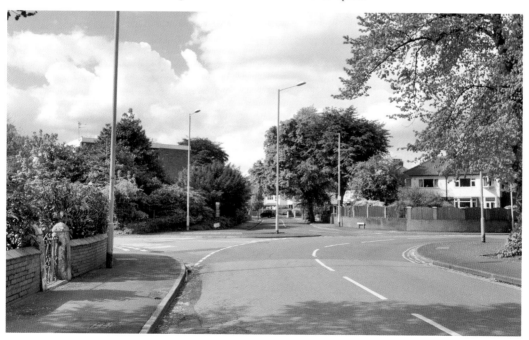

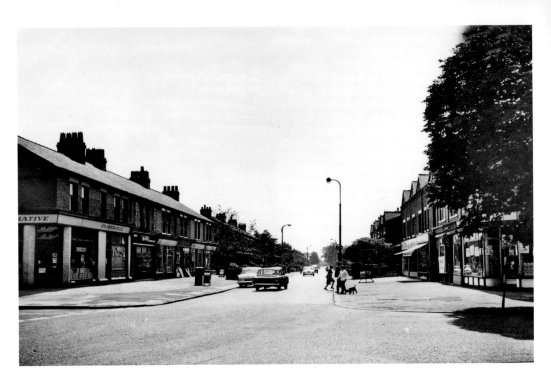

**Moorside Road, 1960 and 2013**

This view from the 1960s shows the northern end of Moorside Road flanked by two supermarkets, where a charity shop and Italian restaurant now stand. The paved area outside the shops has yet to be cut back to accommodate parking bays for increased traffic, and the postbox is still in its original position outside the post office, which opened in the 1930s. Although traffic is starting to increase, it poses little threat to the pedestrian and her dog.

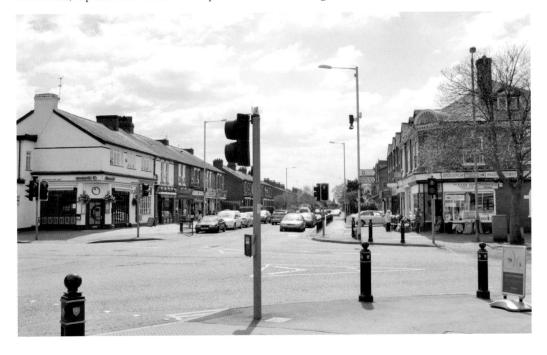

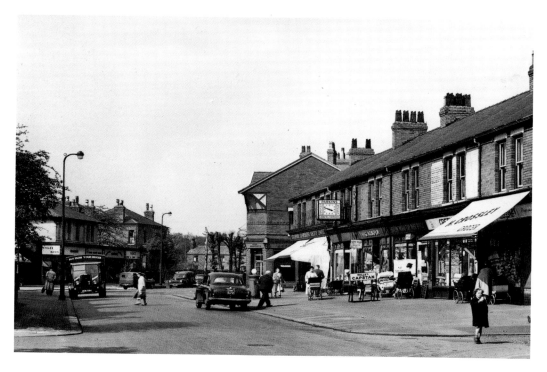

## Moorside Road, 1967 and 2013

A busy scene from 1967! It is ten to four, and a child meanders home from school, having doubtless been guided across the road by the lollipop man, who can be seen next to the van on the left. Parking and traffic management have not yet become an issue, and the man leaving his car to use the post office is in the minority compared to the number of pedestrians. On Heaton Moor Road, Beech House still stands proudly before its demolition to provide space for a modern supermarket.

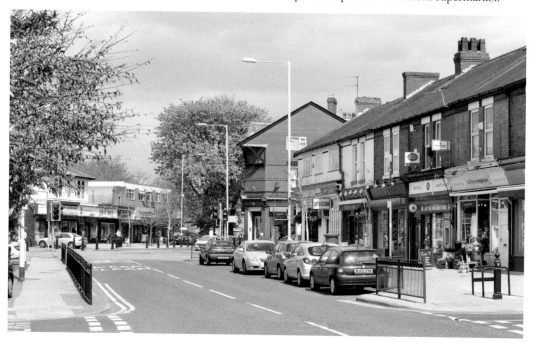

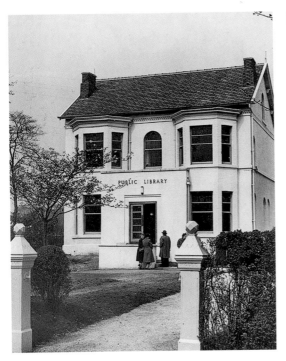
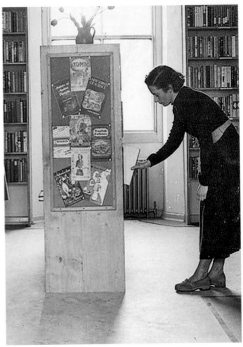

**Heaton Moor Library, 1950 and 2013**
Moor House, the home of the Barlow family, became Heaton Moor Library in 1950. It was opened on 4 May by Alderman L. B. Lowe. Although it encouraged younger readers, only children over the age of thirteen could use the lending facilities. In 1992, the library moved to its current premises further along Thornfield Road and Moor House reverted to its original purpose as a private residence.

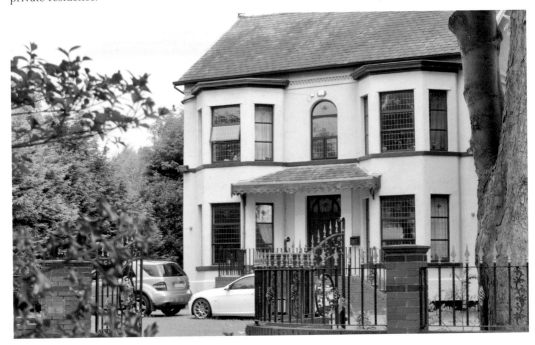

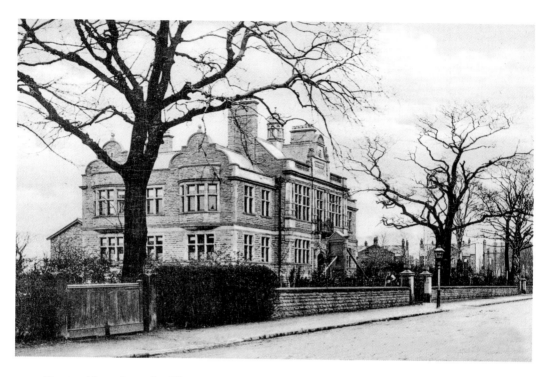

**Heaton Moor Council Offices, 1904 and 2013**

This view has remained largely unchanged since the early part of the twentieth century. The grounds of the council offices are now shared with the new Heatons Library building, and the large Victorian houses, which can be seen on Balmoral Road, were demolished in 1959 and the space used to build the Drs Green & Slater Rest Homes.

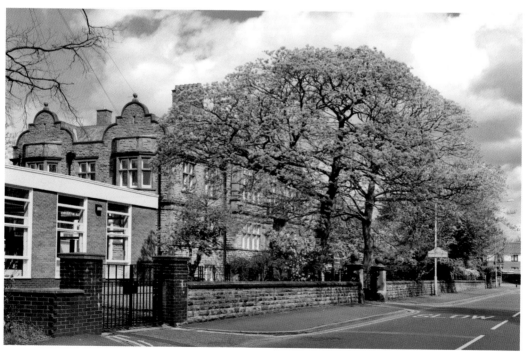

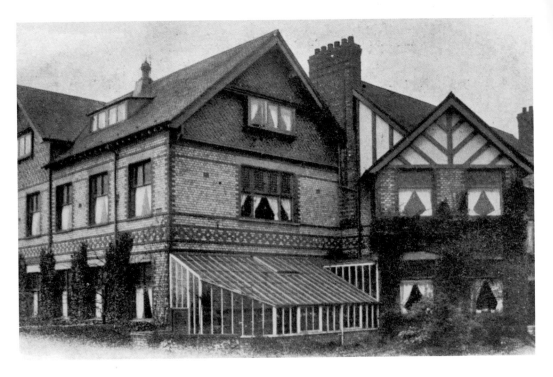

## Fylde Lodge School, 1904 and 2013

Formally a private house, Fylde Lodge School opened in 1893. It was initially an establishment for the daughters of local wealthy families, and offered a curriculum including singing, drawing and needlework. In 1921, the school was taken over by Stockport LEA and became a girls' grammar school serving the local area. The site was sold for housing in the 1990s, but some of the original building was retained to form part of the College Court flats complex.

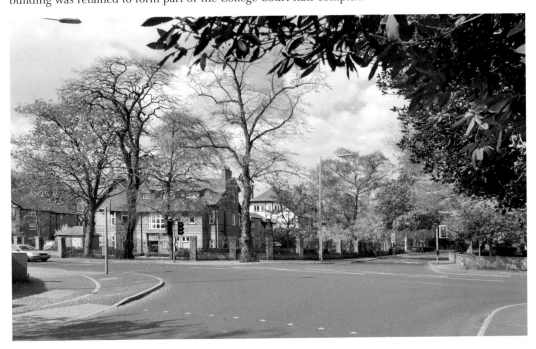

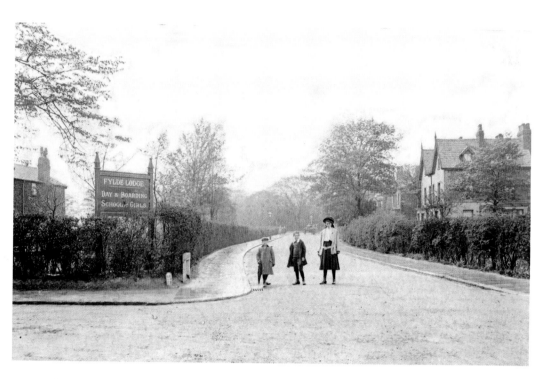

### Fylde Lodge School, 1907 and 2013

This nostalgic photograph shows three children outside Fylde Lodge School posing for the camera. They are separated by at least four generations from the pupils from Priestnall High School, which opened in 1974. They represent a world without cars, aircraft, television, the Internet or mobile phones; children living their lives in a quiet, semi-rural environment, worlds away from the pace of modern teenage life in the twenty-first century.

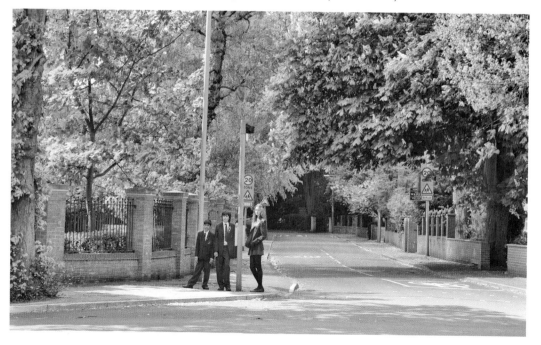

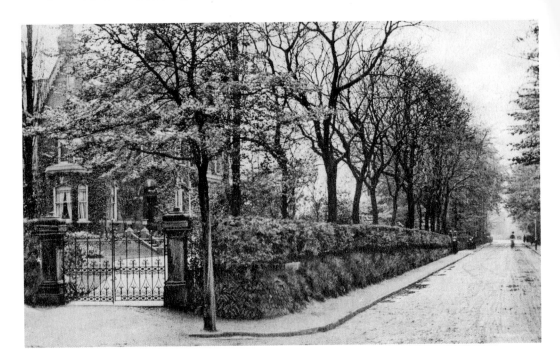

**Thornfield Road, 1903 and 2013**

Matthew Curtis, a local brass founder, built his home, Thornfield, on Didsbury Road, where his family continued to live until sometime after his death in 1887. In the mid-1930s, Thornfield was sold and demolished, but the family and house names live on in the names of the two local roads. This view along Thornfield Road, towards Moor Top, shows a gated entrance to a large house. The building still remains as private housing, with its original grounds forming part of Heaton Moor Park.

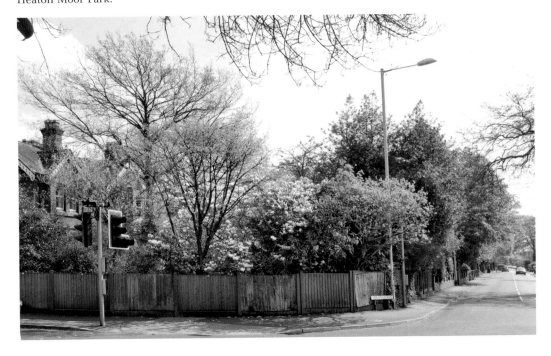

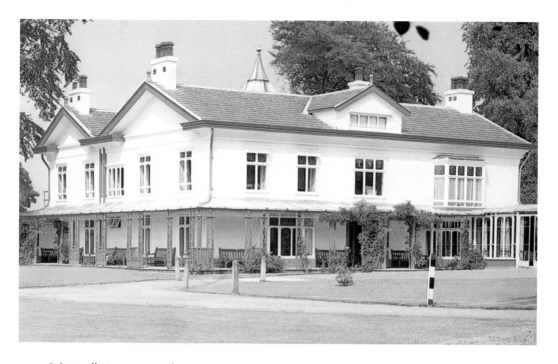

### Priestnall Hey, 1979 and 2013

Priestnall Hey was the home of Swiss entrepreneur Hans Renold. In 1908, he bought several acres of land in the Manchester suburb of Burnage and started the eight-year task of building the largest chain manufacturing plant in his group. Priestnall Hey was situated in the grounds, but was demolished in the early 1980s. The site now comprises of a housing estate, superstore and part of Heaton Mersey common land. The gateposts to the entrance are all that are left of this once magnificent house.

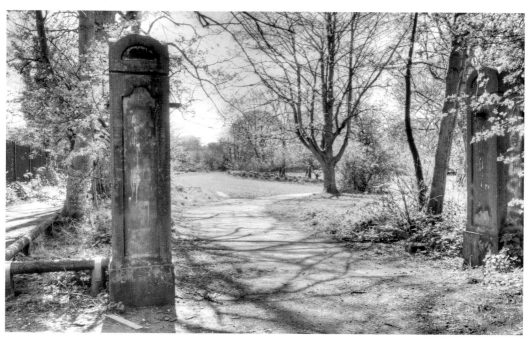

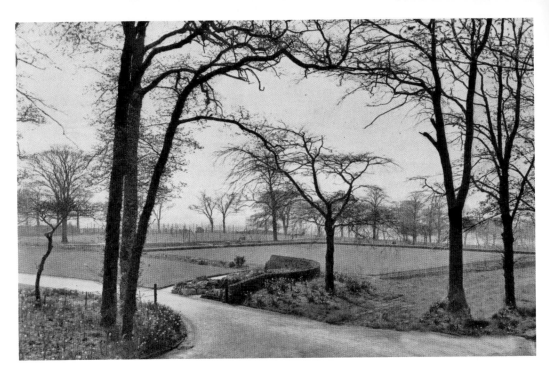

## Hans Renold Recreation Grounds, 1947 and 2013

On 15 May 1948, Hans Renold held the official opening of his new bowling green and tennis courts. It was a grand affair, with a full programme of events including a garden fête, a bowling and tennis tournament, dancing displays and, later in the evening, a smoking concert in the new assembly room on the west side of Priestnall Hey. The land is still mostly open common ground, and the pattern of the trees in the foreground can still be identified.

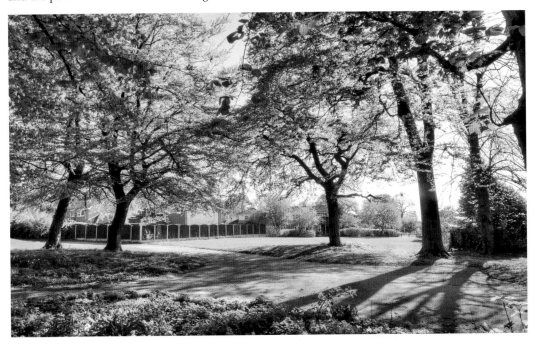

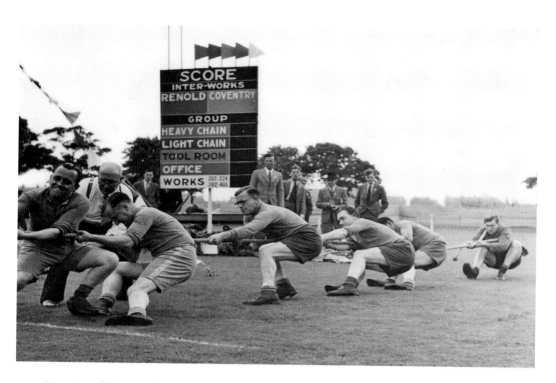

**Hans Renold Sports Day, 1957**

Hans Renold was devoted to the ideal of establishing a firm sense of community among his employees and their families. After the Second World War, he took a significant step in providing increased leisure opportunities for his workers, and regular sports days were an important part of his team building. Renold's competitors sported the Swiss badge on their athletics kit, and events were held on the sports field, which now forms part of the Heaton Mersey Common open land.

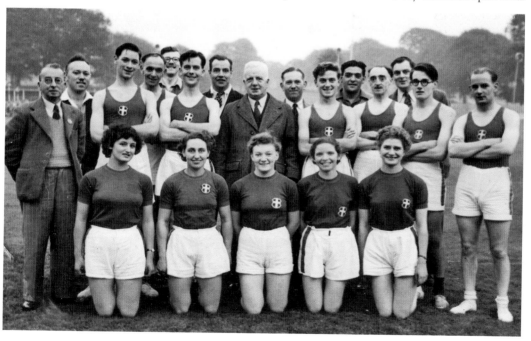

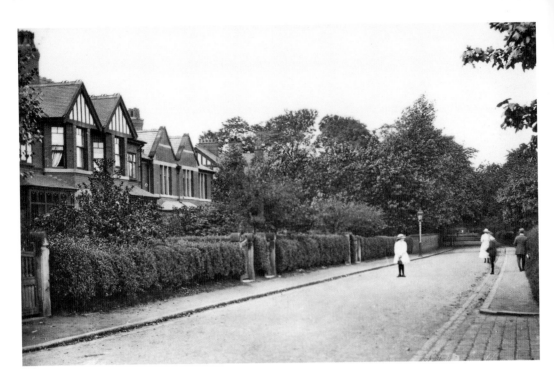

**Mersey Road, 1910 and 2013**

For a long time, Mersey Road was the main pathway between Didsbury Road and Mauldeth Road, exiting near Tithebarn Farm. In 1890, Joseph Padmore acquired land to the southern end of the road, building first a small estate of terraced houses, and later some larger houses to the north of Hawthorn Road. The first two houses on the left of the modern picture were finished in 1908 and had an initial selling price of £500.

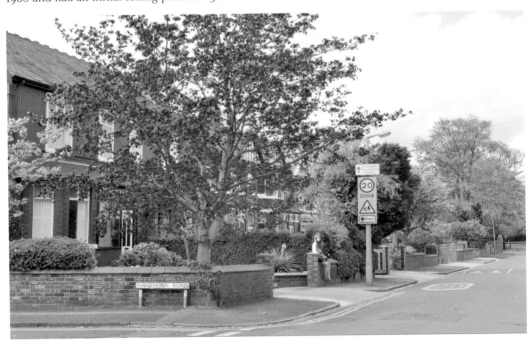

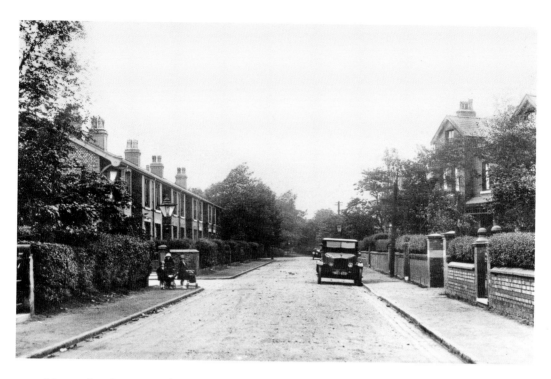

**Mersey Road, 1920s and 2013**

Another view of Mersey Road from the 1920s. The car in the foreground is probably a Ford Model T Tourer. By the start of the decade, it had been in production for eleven years, and was a popular vehicle with the new motoring classes. It had a top speed of 40 mph, retailed for around £200 and was assembled locally in Manchester. Today, the road is lined with traffic humps and bollards to safeguard children from the local schools at busy times.

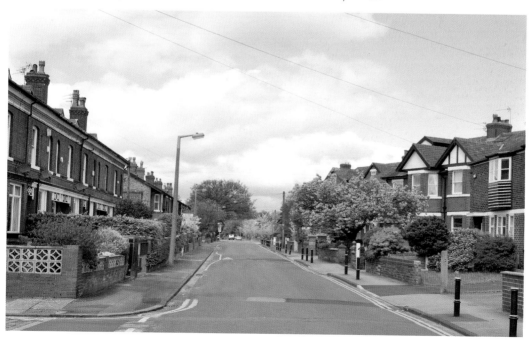

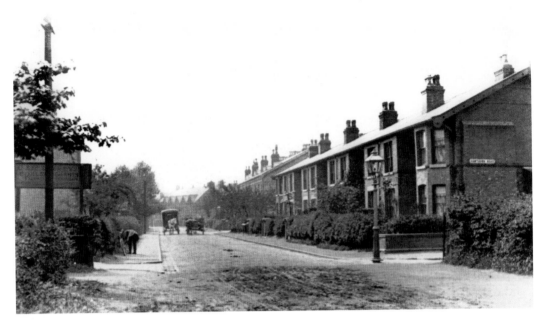

**Cephas Linney's Coalyard and Mersey Villas, 1904 and 1992**
This postcard from 1904 shows the entrance to Cephas Linney's coalyard on Mersey Road. Cephas built the first houses on the east side of the road in 1891, naming them Mersey Villas. He ran his business from home, keeping his horses and carts in stabling behind the house. The stabling still remained until 1992, when the site was cleared for modern housing. The Linneys have a family grave in the grounds of the congregational church on Mersey Road.

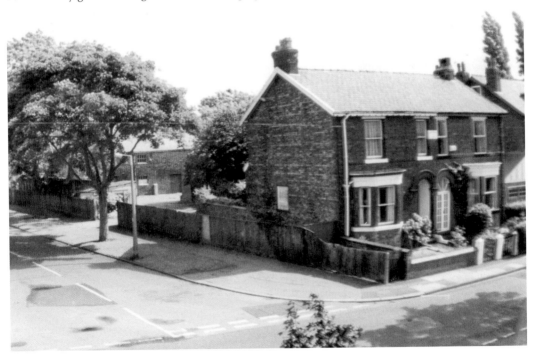

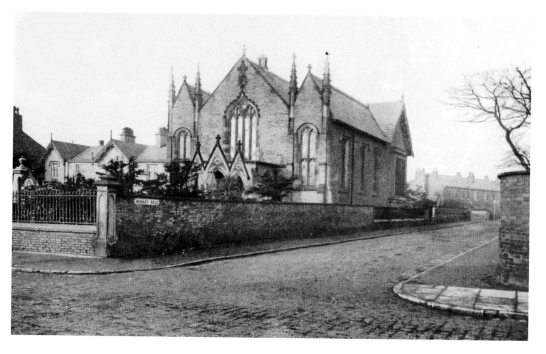

## Congregational Church, Mersey Road, 1880 and 2013

The church was built around 1840 to accommodate a growing congregation, who were probably worshipping in the converted front room of one of the cottages on Vale Road. Over the next quarter of a century, the church buildings were extended and rooms added to the north to cater for the demand for a Sunday school. The main church building became infested with dry rot and was demolished in 1988. The graveyard was moved to the grounds of the church hall behind the modern flats.

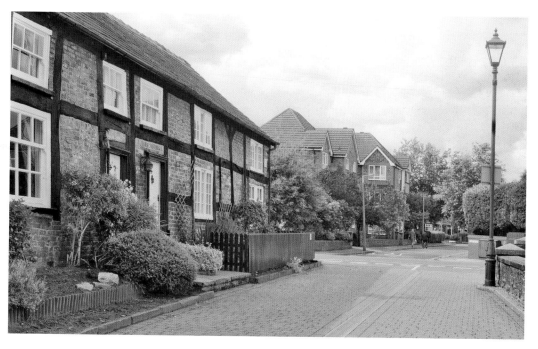

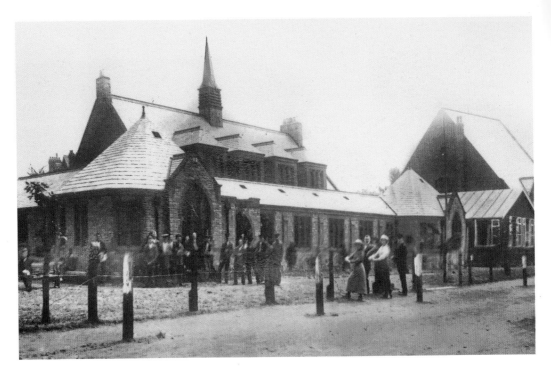

### The Red Cross Hospital, 1918 and 2013

The Heatons had two wartime hospitals, one in Heaton Moor at the Reform Club, and this one on Cavendish Road in Heaton Mersey, which closed in March 1919. It ran under the leadership of Walter Brownsword, a teacher who was too old to enlist but keen to help the war effort. The wards were run by VAD (Voluntary Aid Detachment) nurses, while Walter and his men met special trains and conveyed the injured to the hospital.

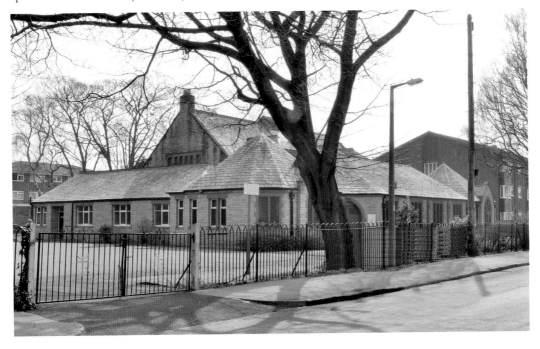

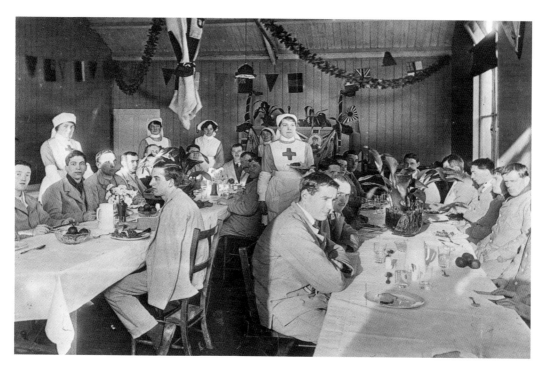

**The Red Cross Hospital Dining Room, 1918, and Cavendish Road, 1930s**

The soldiers recovering in the Red Cross Hospital may have enjoyed a stroll up Cavendish Road as part of their recuperation. Cavendish Road was an unmade residential street until as late as the 1970s, and is characterised at its northern end by a mixture of housing from the turn of the century and the interwar houses of the 1930s. The far end of the road, near the hospital, marks the location of Alegar Fold, a long-established settlement that appears on the earliest maps of the area but was cleared in 1891.

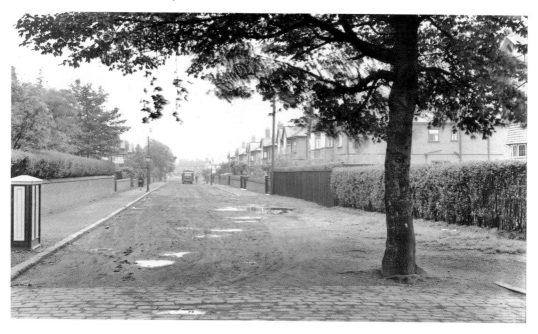

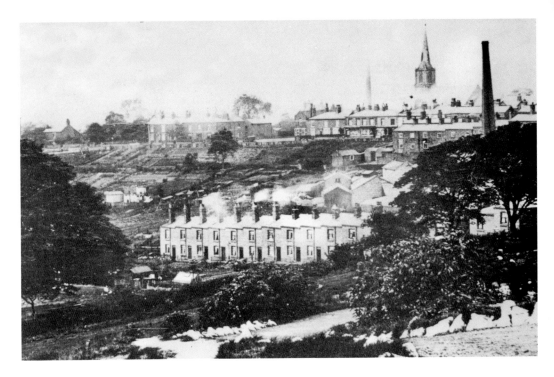

**Park Row and Park Place, 1880s and 2013**

The enclave of houses forming Park Row and Park Place was built on land originally owned by Robert Parker, proprietor of the Upper Bleach Works. The houses in Park Row were probably built after his death by the next owner of the Bleach Works, Samuel Stocks, and date from around 1830. The houses are built on a steep incline and each has its own allotment-type garden opposite the front door.

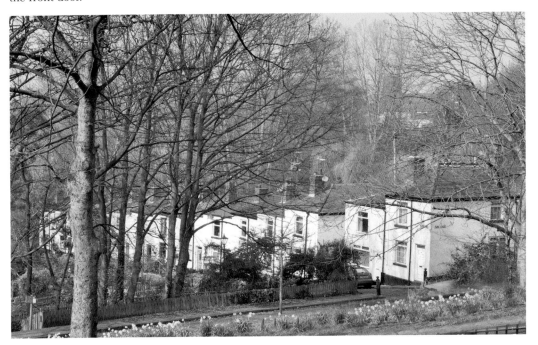

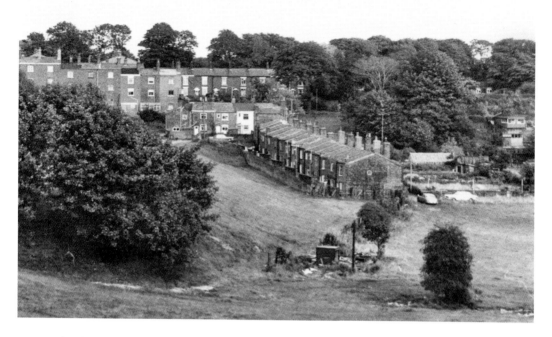

## Vale Close and Park Row, 1970s and 2013

In 1785, Samuel Oldknow, a cloth manufacturer, established a bleaching, printing and dyeing works on the banks of the River Mersey. Houses were needed for the workers and Park Row, along with Vale Close, was built in the early 1800s. Today, the cottages are sought-after private residences in the Heaton Mersey Conservation Area. The foliage surrounding the cottages now makes getting a rear shot of the terraces virtually impossible.

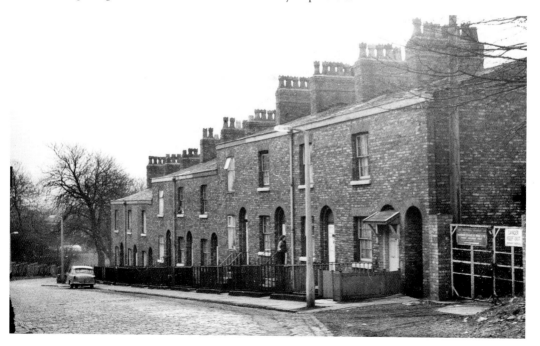

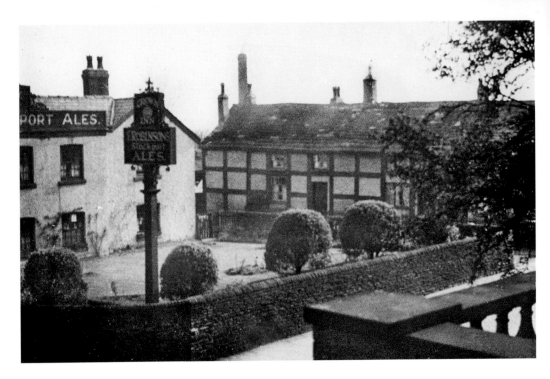

### The Crown Inn and Vale Cottages, 1930 and 2013

The Crown was built around 1700, is a Grade II listed building, and originally consisted of the inn, a stable, a bakehouse and five cottages. The bakehouse produced bread every day, and villagers could take their own bread to be baked in the large ovens on certain days at a charge of a halfpenny per loaf. It acquired its first full licence around 1830, but was not fully modernised until the twentieth century. The old photograph is taken from the terrace of Parr's House, a large villa, which occupied the ground now taken for modern housing.

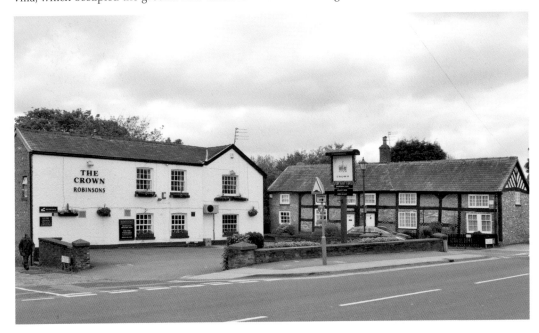

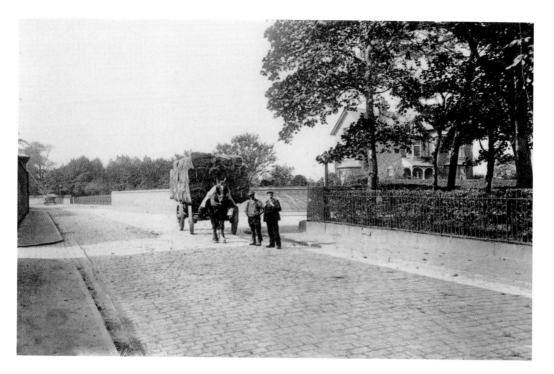

### Didsbury/Mauldeth Junction, 1908 and 2013

Mauldeth Road was originally the main route connecting Burnage with Didsbury. This quiet scene, at the junction with Didsbury Road, is unrecognisable as today's busy thoroughfare, which handles large amounts of traffic each day. Hardly any houses exist, and the top of the congregational church on Mersey Road can just be made out in the distance. The attractive Victorian house on the corner has since been demolished and replaced by the Highbury flats complex.

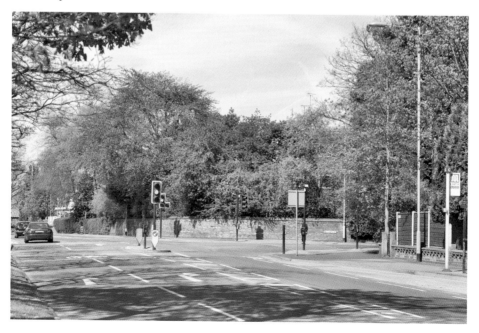

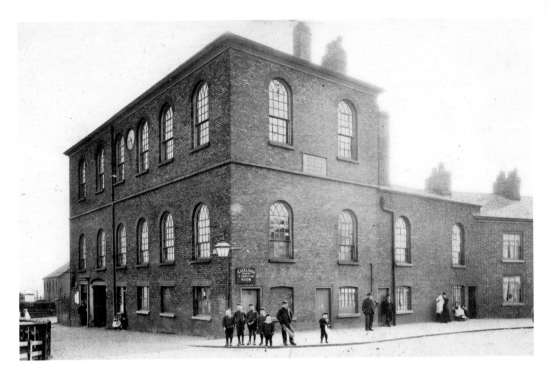

**Heaton Mersey Sunday School, 1890 and 2013**
Heaton Mersey Sunday School provided religious education and classes in reading and writing for over 300 pupils in the mid- to late 1800s. Between 1862 and 1863, industries in the area were badly hit by the restriction of cotton bale imports from the USA, due to the American Civil War, and the school was used for meetings of the local relief committee to help workers who were laid off from local factories. The area was cleared for modern housing in the 1970s.

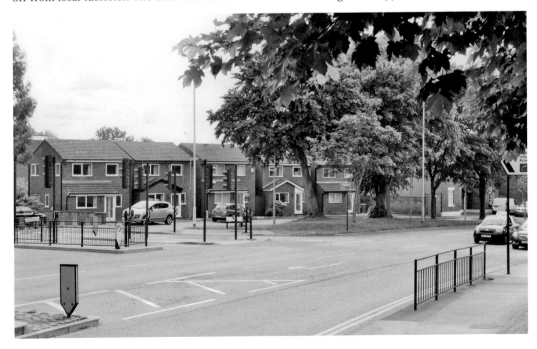

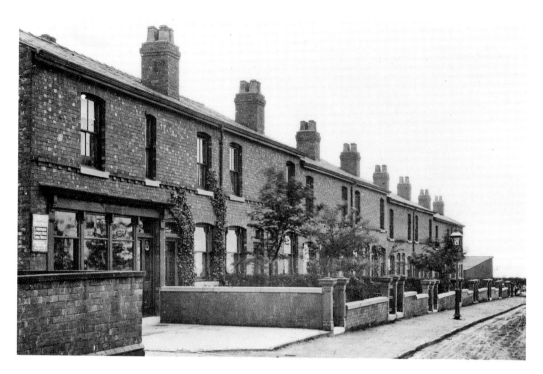

## Hawthorn Road, 1907 and 2013

Hawthorn Road is the last of the 'tree' streets running west off Mersey Road, the others being New Beech, Lyme and Poplar. The houses were constructed by local builder Joseph Padmore, who is buried in the graveyard of the congregational church on Mersey Road. Each road had its own shop at the end of the row, and the inset picture shows the last surviving one, which closed in the early 1990s.

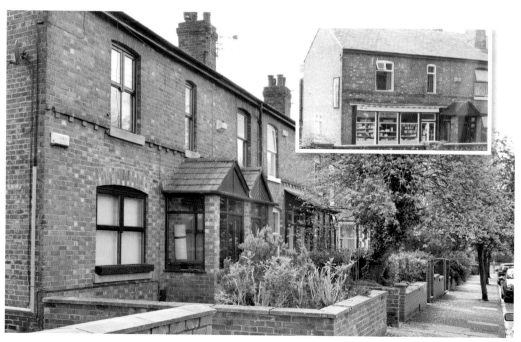

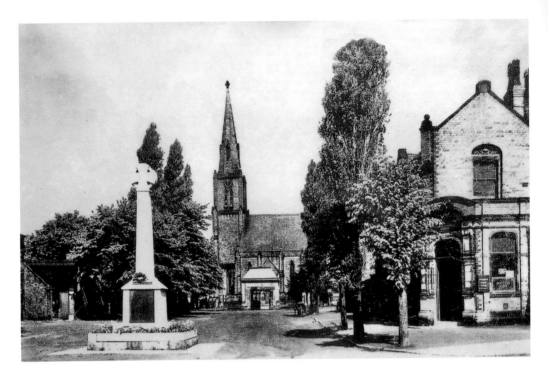

**St John's, Heaton Mersey, 1930 and 2013**

The church of St John the Baptist is a Grade II listed building, built in early Gothic style with an interior gallery and boxed pews. There are a number of interesting buildings surrounding the church, including the parish hall, Stella Maris School and the former schoolmaster's house. Originally, the church had a 125-foot spire, but this had to be removed for safety reasons in 1995 and was replaced with the current parapet and pinnacles.

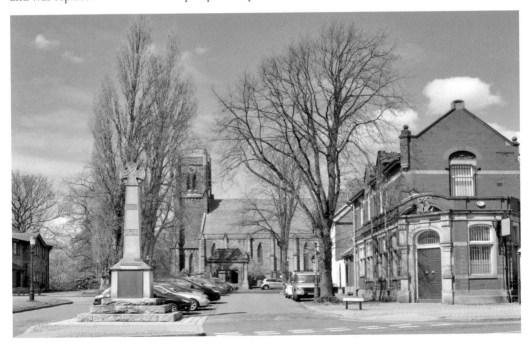

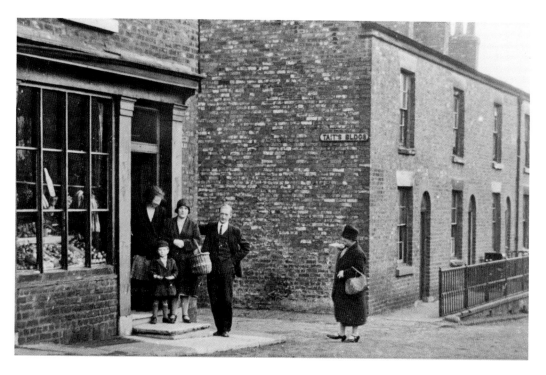

**Vale Road and Tait's Buildings, 1950s and 2013**

A view of the corner of Vale Road and Tait's Buildings showing the corner shop, which was a feature of many of the streets around the Heatons right up until the 1990s. Tait's Buildings were two rows of back-to-back houses built by Mortimer Lavater Tait, who managed the Lower Bleach Works in the mid-1880s. They were built using the bricks of a demolished chimney and provided accommodation for his workers, including those who came from orphanages and the workhouses.

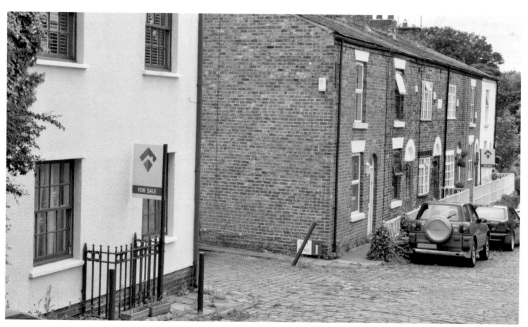

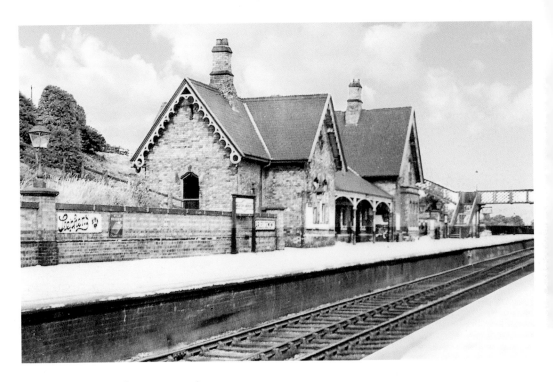

## Heaton Mersey Station, 1950s and 2013

Heaton Mersey station was opened in the 1880s and had two staff: Mr Little, the stationmaster, and Mr Swift, the porter. The station was owned by the Cheshire Lines Committee and was built in a style that reflected their railway station design. The Trans-Pennine Trail footpath follows the line of the railway from Parrs Wood to Station Road. The northern section of the line still exists and has recently reopened as a modern tram route into the city.

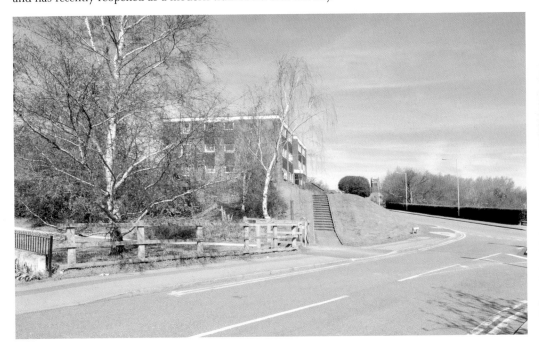

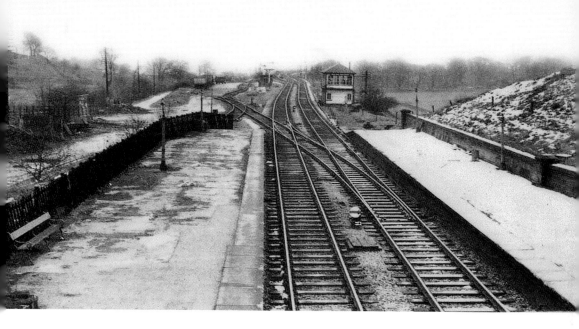

**Heaton Mersey Station, 1960 and 1983**

The line ran from Manchester through to Derby and the Peak Forest on the Midland route. The station was located in a shallow cutting and was reached by a long, sloping path from Didsbury Road, which led to a strangely-shaped footbridge that was part of the public right of way. This view is taken from the footbridge looking towards Stockport. The station was closed in July 1961, and by 1983 only a single line was left to succumb to rust and weeds.

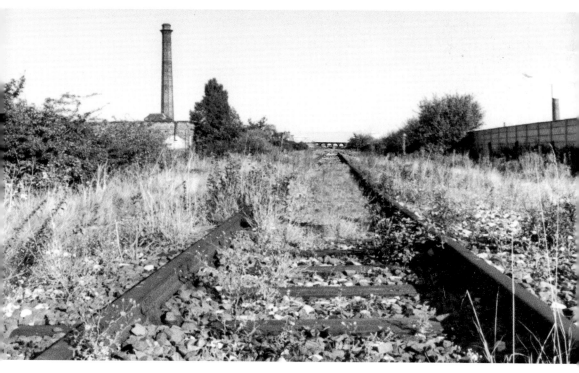

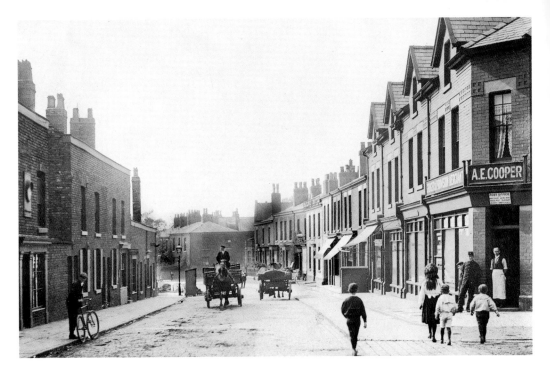

**Didsbury Road, 1907 and 2013**

The buildings on the left formed a double row of shops and residential houses with cellars that connected to the premises on the opposite side of the road. At one time there were over forty businesses located on this small stretch of road, but many were demolished when Didsbury Road was widened in the 1970s. The shop on the corner was built and owned by Alfred Cooper, and doubled as a grocer's and post office.

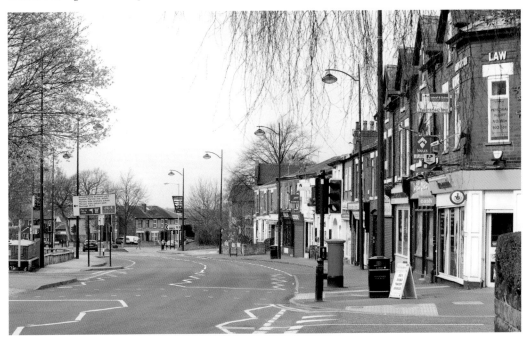

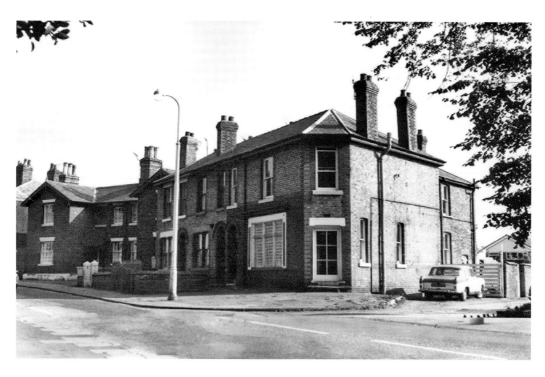

## Didsbury Road Police Station, 1974 and 2013

In the mid-nineteenth century, Heaton Mersey had a number of constables from the Lancashire County Constabulary based at the police station on Didsbury Road. The station had proper custodial facilities, replacing the lock-up in Heaton Place, which held offenders temporarily, quite often in the view of the passing public. By 1913, the cells were no longer needed and the building was turned into two police houses. The last police occupant left in 1961.

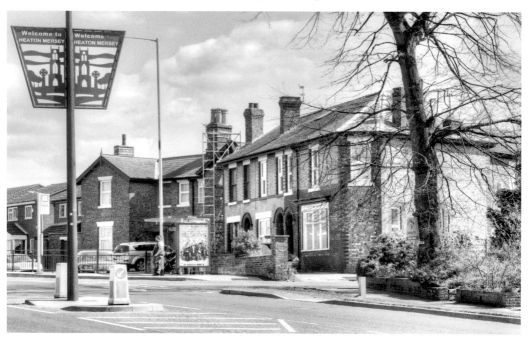

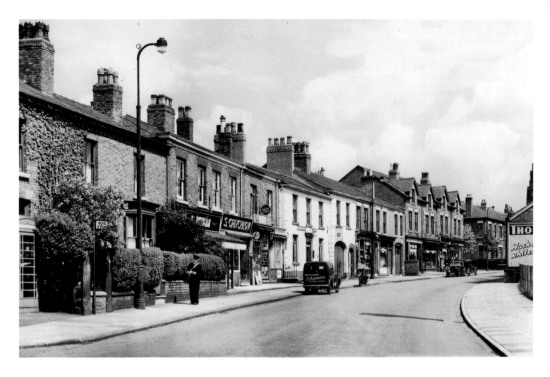

### Didsbury Road, 1960 and 2013

This quiet view of Didsbury Road from the 1960s shows the Railway Hotel and a range of shops supplying the needs of local people. The van belongs to Critchlow's, the butcher, which is flanked on either side by Brown's fruit shop and a newsagent. Further up is a baker's shop, an electrical shop and the post office. The buildings opposite the post office also accommodated businesses, including another newsagent and a sweet shop.

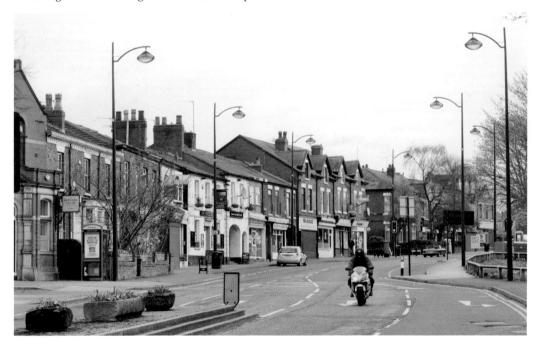

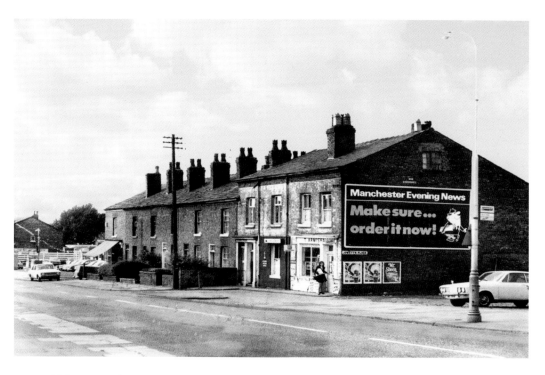

## Didsbury Road, 1970 and 2013

This row of shops, including Armishaw's newsagents, stretched from the petrol station to the Griffin Pub. The whole row was demolished during the 1970s, and the scene today is altogether more green and welcoming than the run-down feel of the '70s. The entrance to Jowett's Place still remains, but leads only into the large pub car park.

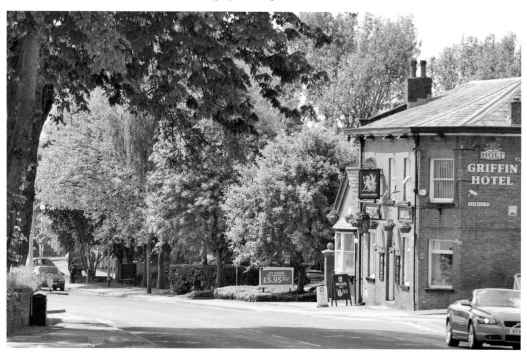

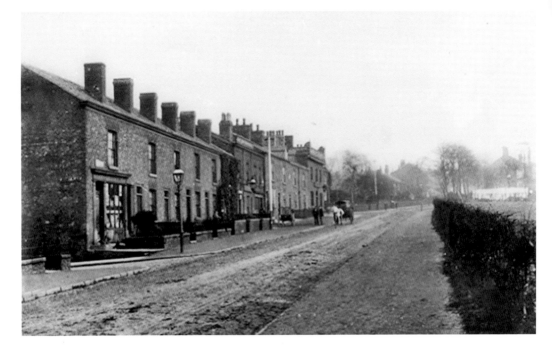

**Didsbury Road, 1910 and 2013**

This view east along Didsbury Road has lost many of the landmarks that would have been familiar to the travellers in the horse and cart. The line of shops on the east side of Jowett's Place, which formed part of Jersey Place, has been replaced with a car park and extension for the Griffin. Further on, the grounds of Grundy Hill House, owned by the Thorniley family, can be seen behind the wall, and across the road Grundy Hill Farm occupies land that is now used for private housing.

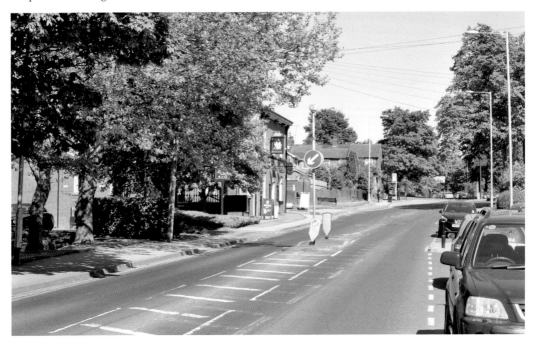

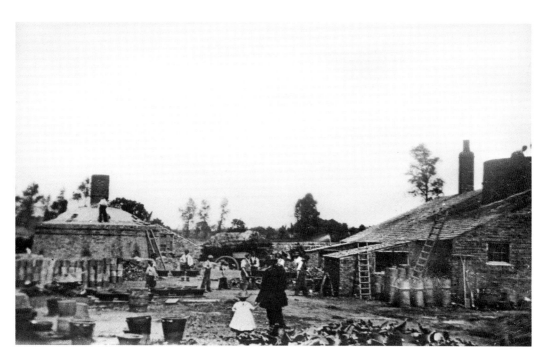

### Heaton Mersey Brickworks, 1930 and 2013

John Thorniley built up his brickwork company making tiles, bricks and pottery for local businesses. The main buildings and the kiln were located on what is now the Crossgate Mews housing development on Harwood Road, near the poplars on the left-hand side of the modern picture. The quarry was situated on land now occupied by Cranford Golf Driving Range and Heaton Mersey Sports and Social Club.

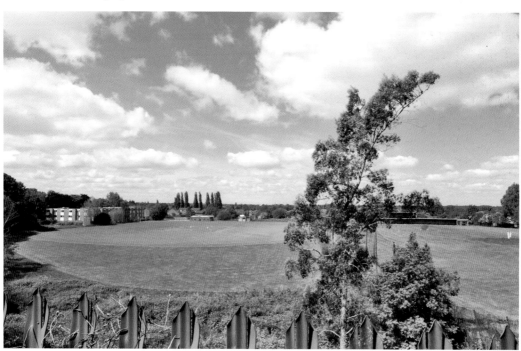

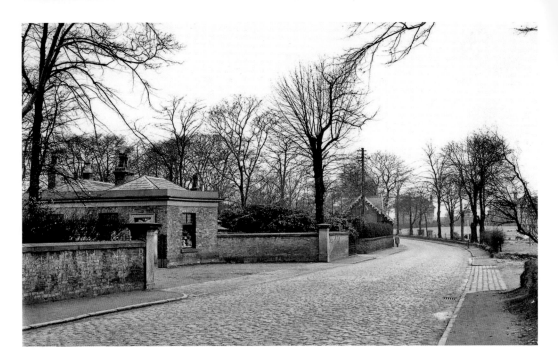

**Didsbury Road, 1930s and 2013**

The photograph shows the entrance to West Bank, one of the imposing residences built on the ridge known as Top o'th'Bank, which gave residents clean fresh air and an unrivalled view of the Cheshire Plain. The road opposite was the entrance to Thornfield, a mansion built by the Curtis family around 1880. The site of West Bank is now occupied by St Winifred's Primary School, but the large stone pillars remain as testament to the home built by Charles H. Scott JP in the mid-1800s.

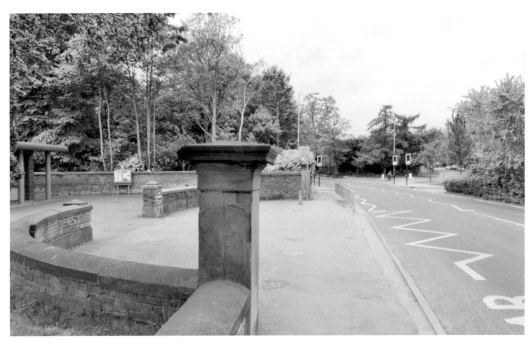

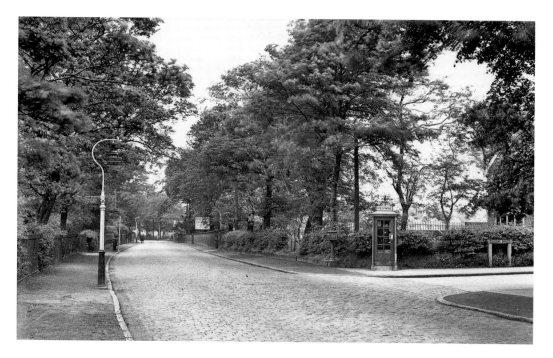

Queens Drive and Didsbury Road Junction, 1920s and 2013

This quiet, leafy scene of the entrance to Queens Drive can be easily dated from the presence of the K1 (Kiosk 1) telephone box, which was introduced to British streets in 1920. It was made of concrete and was mainly white, with bright red window panels and an angular roof. Its unpopular design was short lived, and it was replaced by the iconic, red K2 box, designed by Sir Giles Gilbert Scott, in 1926.

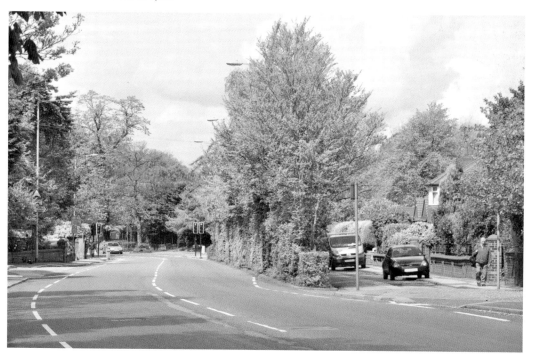

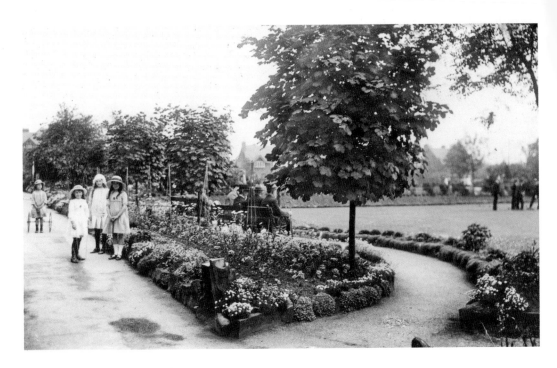

**Heaton Moor Park, 1918 and 2013**

Lord Egerton of Tatton donated approximately 4 acres of land to Heaton Norris District Council in 1894, which resulted in free land on which the local residents could play and enjoy recreational activities. Heaton Moor Park was officially opened on 17 July 1897 to coincide with Queen Victoria's Diamond Jubilee celebrations. The park is now supported by the Friends of the Park organisation, which regularly holds events and fundraising activities to maintain it as an attractive local amenity.

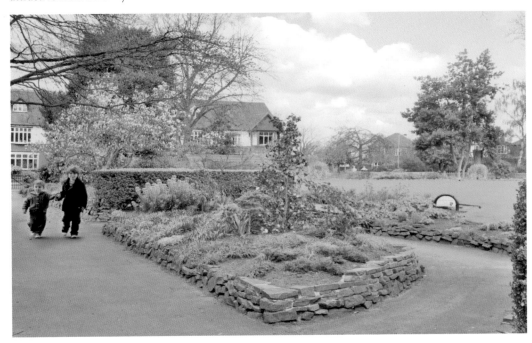

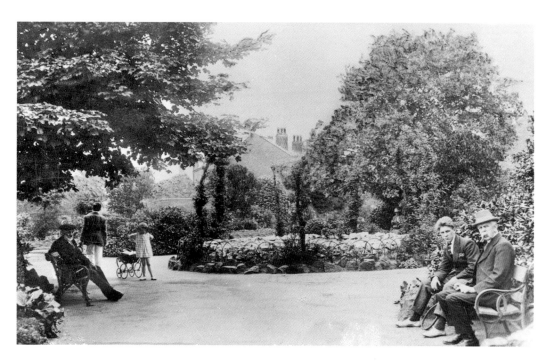

**Heaton Mersey Park, 1927 and 2013**

The Industrial Revolution resulted in a substantial rise in the population of Heaton Mersey, as people moved into the area to supply labour for the brickmaking, bleaching and dyeing industries. Heaton Mersey Park was developed around 1880 in an open space with panoramic views over the Cheshire Plain, and incorporated a bowling green, bandstand and tree-lined walks. Today, the park is supported by Heaton Mersey Village Conservation Group, who organise regular family events and farmers' markets.

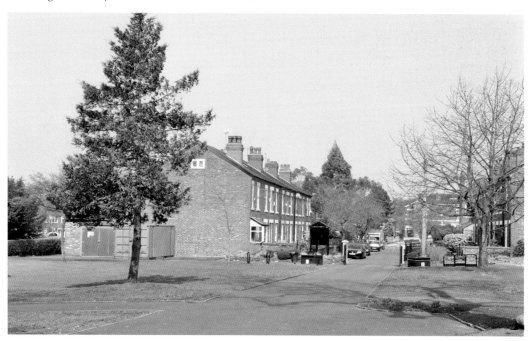

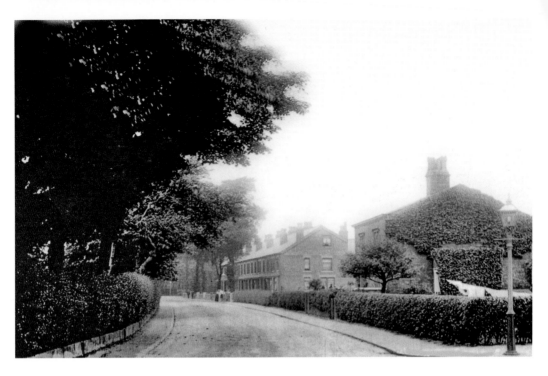

**Bank Hall Road, 1907 and 2013**

At the beginning of the twentieth century, Bank Hall Road was part of an important thoroughfare linking Didsbury Road to Heaton Moor Road and Manchester Road in Heaton Chapel. When the Stockport Corporation expanded its bus network in 1922, the northern end of Bank Hall Road, with its wide turning circle, was the southern terminus for its fleet of Vulcan single-deckers, linking Heaton Moor to Reddish.

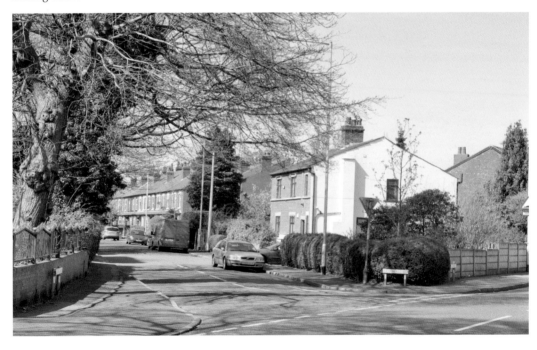

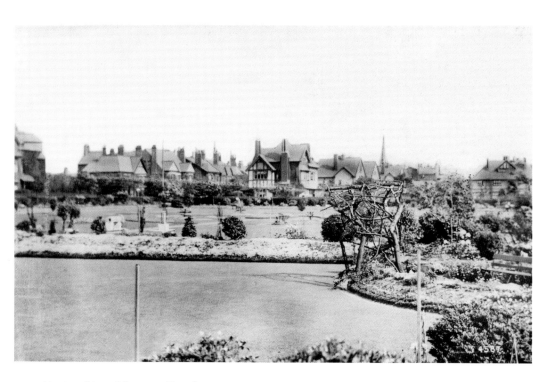

**Heaton Moor View, 1908 and 2013**

This view from across the park has been completely masked by foliage over the years. The old photograph gives a clear view of the wealthy Victorian housing along Peel Moat Road and a fine example of a grand villa, typical of those built within easy reach of the railway station, on the corner of Elms Road. The landscaped features of the park are altogether more open, and allow a view over the moor to St Paul's church on Heaton Moor Road.

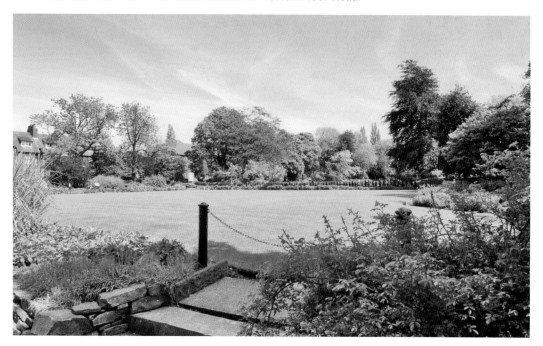

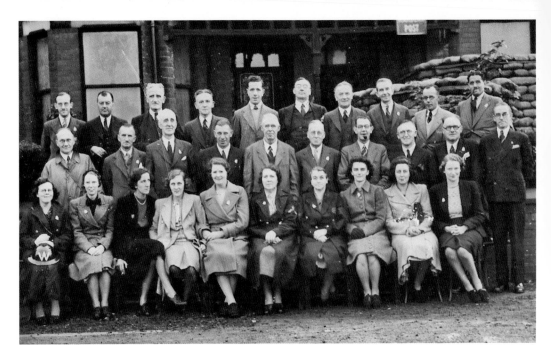

**Brownsville Road ARP Station, 1941 and 2013**

The group would have been responsible for the issuing of gas masks, organising pre-fabricated air-raid shelters, and enforcing the blackout in Heaton Moor. They would have been well-trained in first aid and procedures for treating civilian casualties. Their station is provided with a good barrier of sandbags as protection from bomb blasts. Fortunately, air raids were limited, but the Fairey Aviation factory at Heaton Chapel was one of the major targets during the air raid of 8 May 1941.

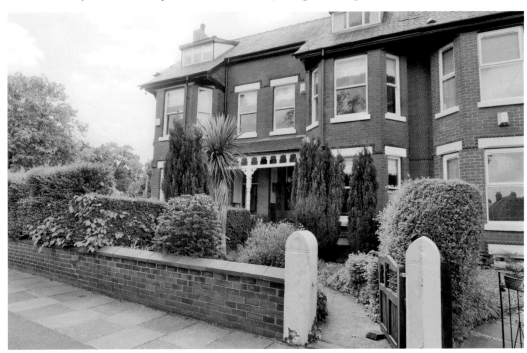

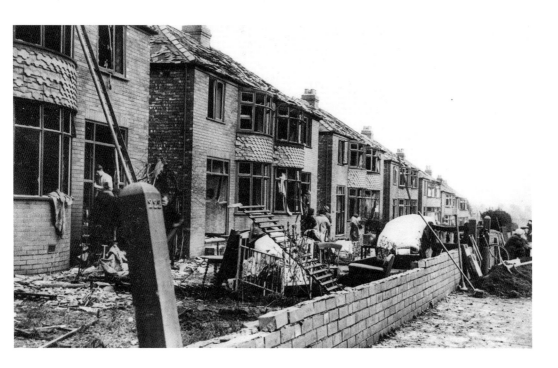

**Bomb Damage, Didsbury Road, 1940 and 2013**

The damage to the houses on Didsbury Road was caused by a landmine, which fell in the nearby grounds of the Alice Briggs' Remand Home. The house of Marion Harris, nearby, in Ryde Avenue, was completely destroyed but she escaped unscathed. Stockport was first bombed on 11 October 1940, but this bombing occurred during the night of 22 December in the same year. The houses were rebuilt and have stood the test of time since the war.

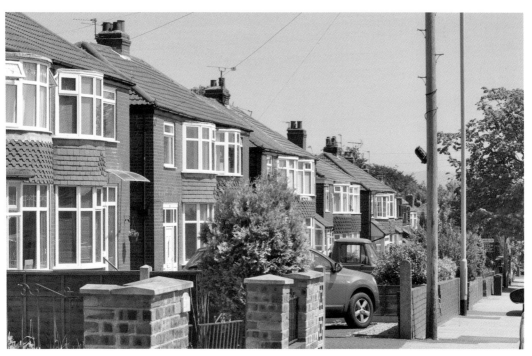

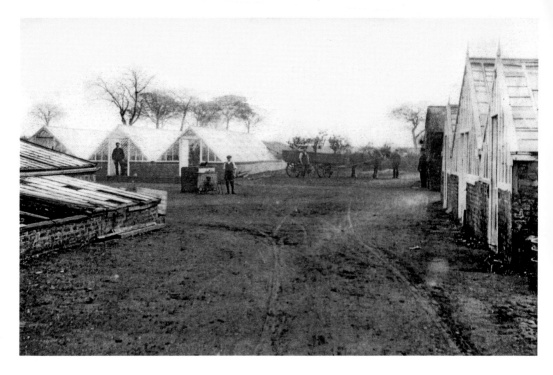

**Green Lane Nursery, 1910 and 2013**
Much of the agricultural land that formed the Heatons has been built upon over the last century. However, there is still a thriving allotment association in the Heatons, and also across Stockport, with over thirty sites. These provide the participants with home-grown vegetables, a social life and the kind of healthy outdoor activity which Heatons' residents of a century ago would also have appreciated.

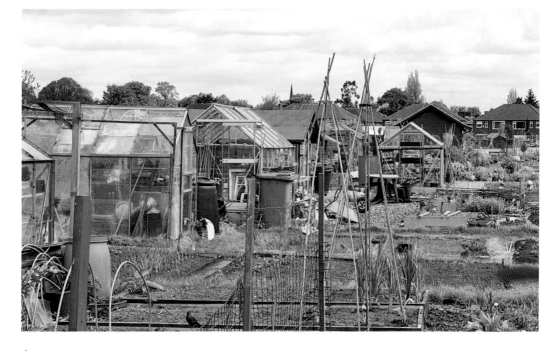

64

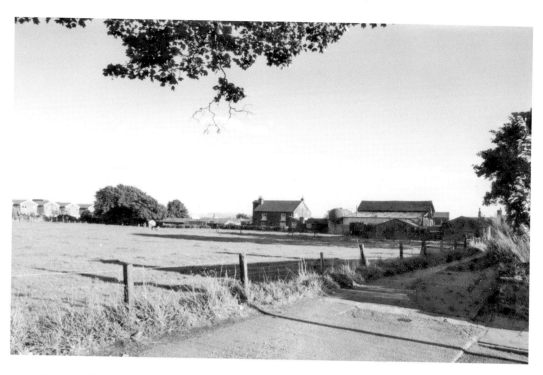

### Norris Hill Farm, 1983 and 2013

Heaton Norris remained agricultural land, especially around Norris Hill and Norris Bank, during the late 1700s and through the 1800s. In fact, a farm had been on this land since the mid-1700s. The Ordnance Survey map of 1908 shows that there were many smaller farms still working the land, along with the Silver Pan Fruit Preserving Works. The lane shown in the 1983 photograph is now a footpath leading around a new housing estate to Didsbury Road.

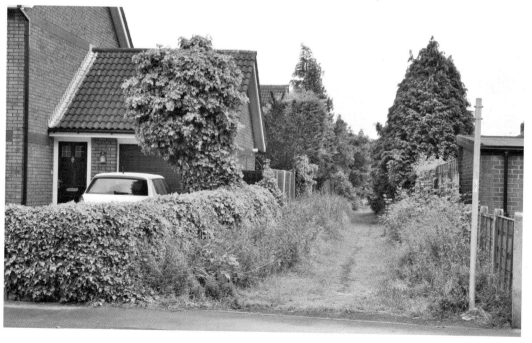

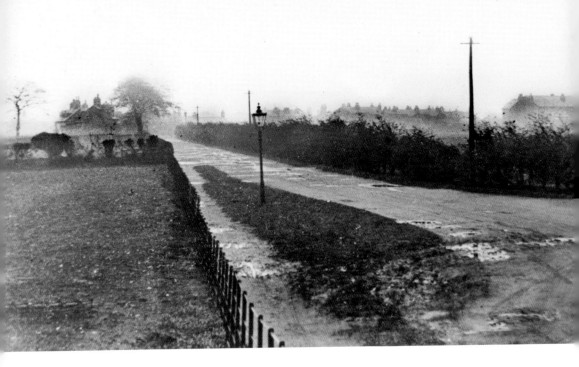

**Green Lane, c. 1900 and 2013**
The agricultural land and muddy lanes that passed through Heaton Norris have been transformed through the years. At the time of the old photograph, Green Lane was a classic example of just how difficult it must have been to get around in the early 1900s. Walking or driving down the lane towards the almshouses is not so difficult today.

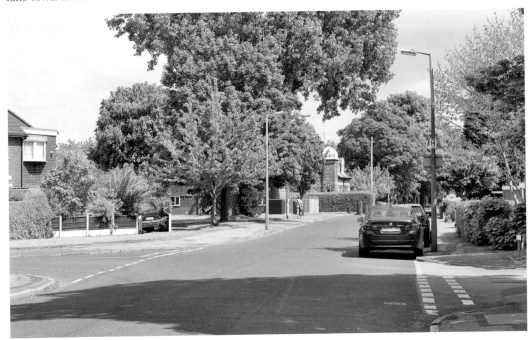

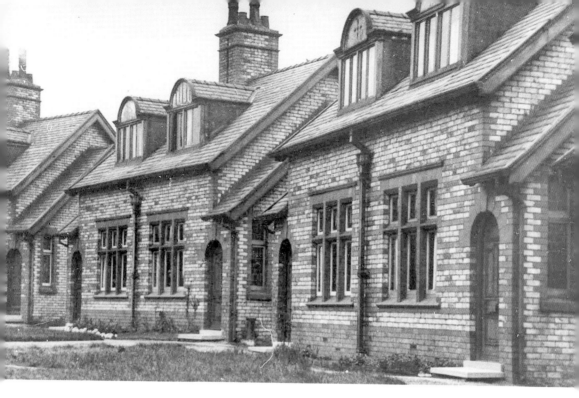

**Almshouses, Green Lane, 1935 and 2013**

The almshouses were a gift from Mr James Ainsworth of Heaton Norris. The Grade II listed buildings were built by Pierce and Son in 1907, and the red and grey brick design, with red terracotta dressings, is very distinctive. There are twelve properties, with both end houses having corner turrets with lead domes.

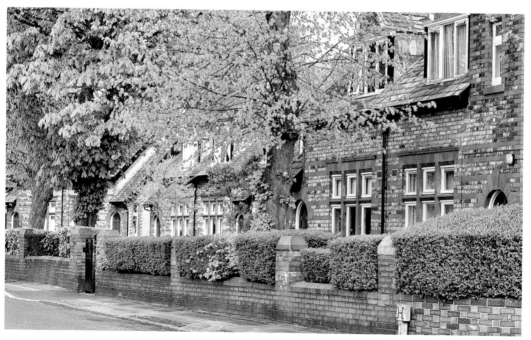

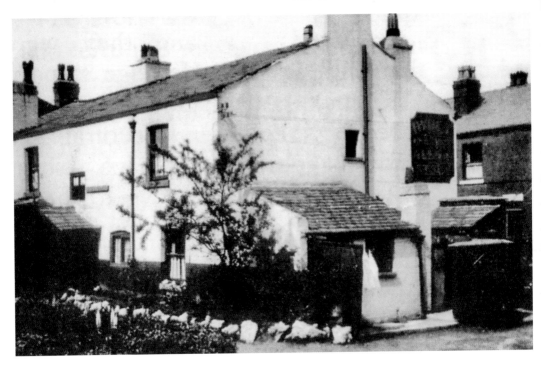

**The Nursery Inn, Green Lane, c. 1910**
Edith Cuthbert lived on Green Lane near the Nursery Inn and worked in the box office at Stockport's Theatre Royal. It was there that she met, and eventually married, a comedian while he was playing the pantomime season in 1888. His name was Frederick John Westcott, better known by his stage name Fred Karno. Fred visited Heaton Norris many times, and is seen here awarding prizes at a local produce show at the Nursery Inn.

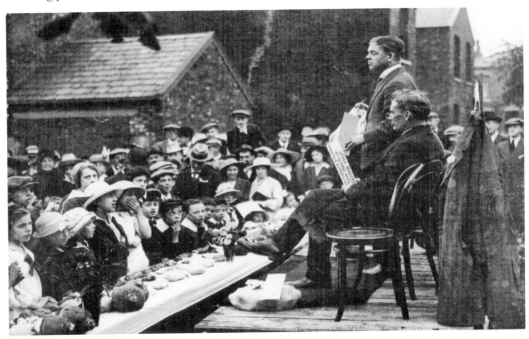

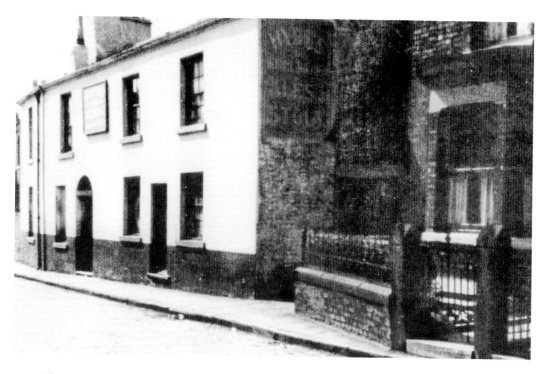

**The Nursery Inn, Green Lane, *c.* 1920 and 2013**

The original public house was built in 1869. Heaton Norris Rovers FC was formed in 1883, and used the pub for their changing rooms. The team played their games on the adjacent football ground. In 1890, the football club changed its name to Stockport County FC, eventually moving south of the River Mersey to Edgeley Park in 1902 as they outgrew the ground and the facilities at the pub. The existing building was built in 1939.

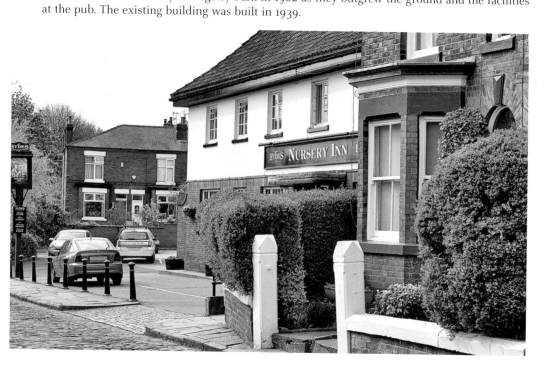

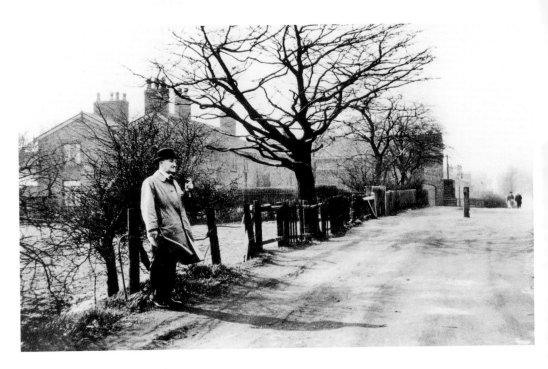

**Bowerfold Lane, *c.* 1900 and 2013**

Bent House Farm was one of several small farms in the Heatons around 1900. The farmland was sold during the 1950s, as land for housing was in demand. However, some of its fields here on Bowerfold Lane have been developed as Bowerfold Open Space. Apart from farming, there were other small, family-owned manufacturing businesses operating in the late 1800s. Robert Harlow moved his boiler-making business to Bowerfold Lane in the mid-1850s. This eventually closed in 1966.

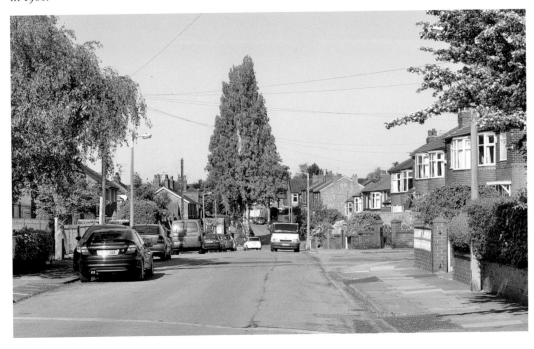

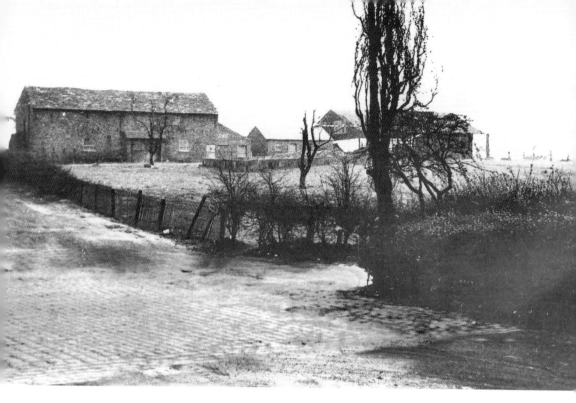

**Bowerhouse Fold, *c.* 1930 and 2013**
Bent House Farm, also known as Bowerhouse Fold, was run by the Melling family. There was a toll route between Wellington Road and Green Lane across the Mellings' land, providing the family with extra income. The farm closed during the 1950s, and the land was sold and developed into a residential area.

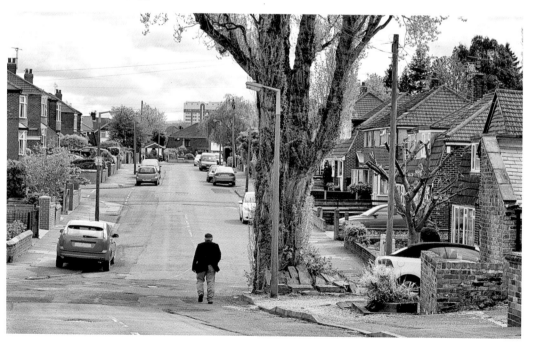

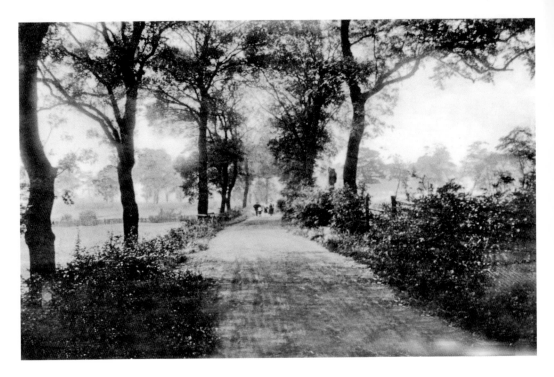

### Craig Road, 1905 and 2013

Craig Road is shown as an unmade lane in the photograph, and also on local Heaton Mersey Village maps, *c.* 1894. Heaton Mersey station was in existence at the time, and Craig Road provided footpath access to both the lower ends of Station Road and Vale Road. Craig Road now links Didsbury Road, below Norris Bank, to Station Road, providing access to new residential areas and the industrial estate.

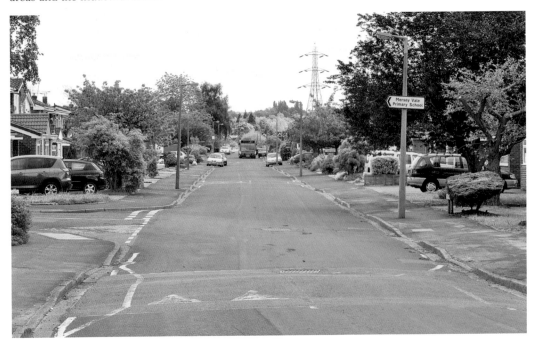

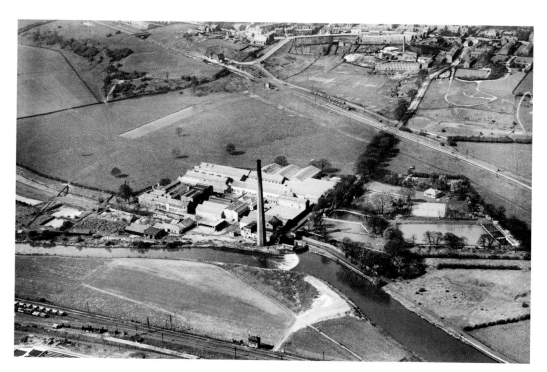

**The Bleach Works, 1927 and 2013**
The Lower Bleach Works in Heaton Mersey was dependent on the water provided by the River Mersey, and an impressive view of the factory is shown in the aerial photograph. The weir and cut can be seen in the centre of the photograph, and the weir is still a feature at this point on the river. A new industrial estate, called the Embankment, has been built on the site once owned by Samuel and Thomas Oldknow.

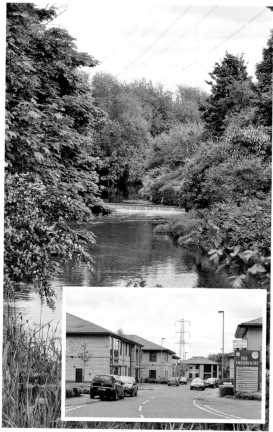

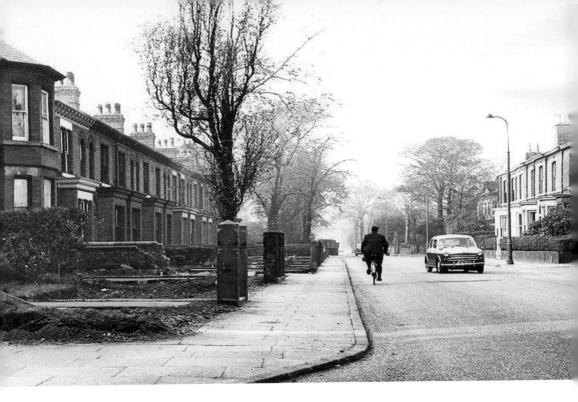

**Didsbury Road, 1962 and 2013**

Didsbury Road, the A5145, is the main route through Heaton Norris and Heaton Mersey. It links Stockport to Didsbury, eventually becoming Wilmslow Road at Parrs Wood. The road itself has been through many changes but the houses have not, apart from losing part of their front gardens due to the widening of the road in the 1960s and '70s.

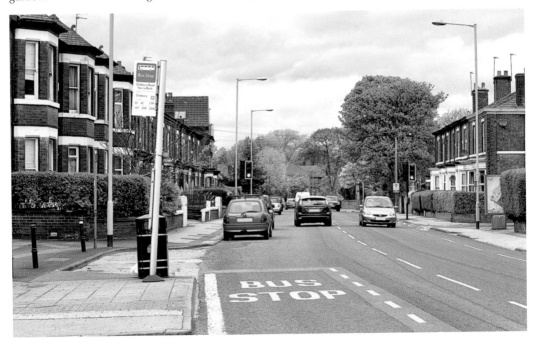

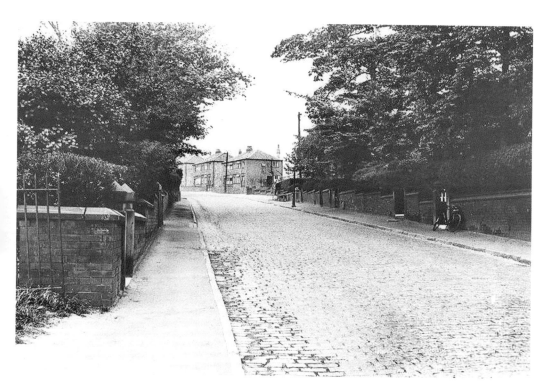

**Norris Bank, Didsbury Road, _c._ 1920 and 2013**
Many of the roads in and around the Heatons were mainly leafy, cobbled lanes, even though they were main routes feeding other towns and villages. The traffic along Didsbury Road at Norris Bank would have been relatively busy in the early 1900s, being close to Stockport town centre, and having many farms and much industry along its route.

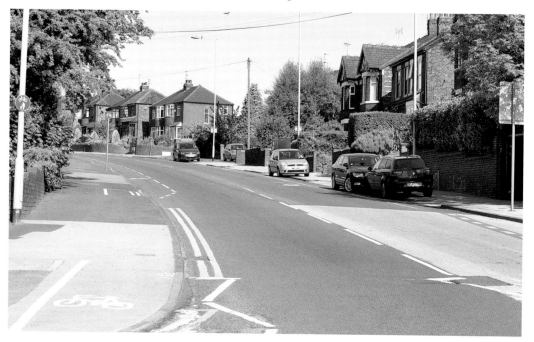

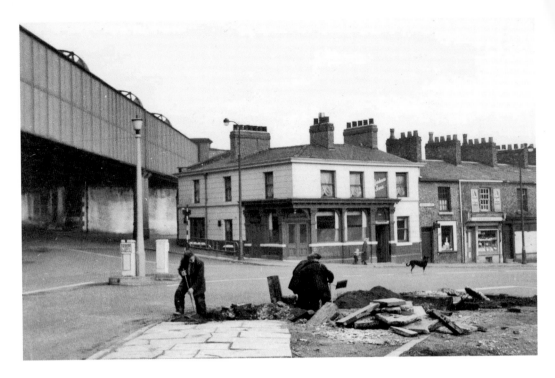

**The Gardener's Arms, c. 1960 and 2013**

The Gardener's Arms public house is shown lying below the line, which was named the Stockport, Timperley and Altrincham Junction Railway. A station, Tiviot Dale, was located nearby at the bottom of Lancashire Hill. The railway tracks and bridge (the bridge supports can still be seen) were dismantled when improvements to the M60 junction were made. Further changes to the area took place when large stores were built along Georges Road.

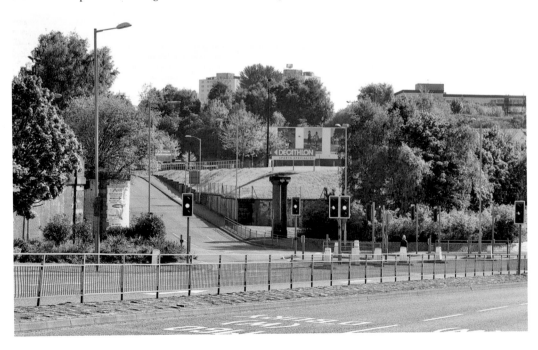

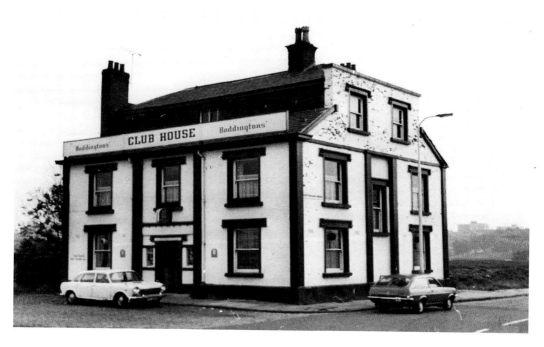

**The Club House, c. 1960 and 2013**

The original licensed house was called the Hat and Feathers, and was built by Francis Phillips around 1825. James Booth later established a brewing business in the pub, with the result that its reputation grew and the brewing facilities had to be enlarged. The name was eventually changed to the Club House, and the Ash Brewery took over the pub in 1865, continuing brewing on the premises until 1893. Large stores now occupy the site, with the iconic Pyramid building close by.

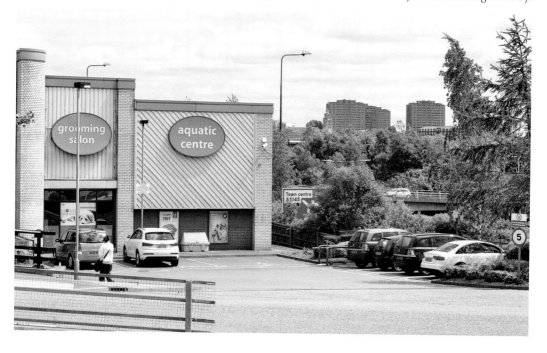

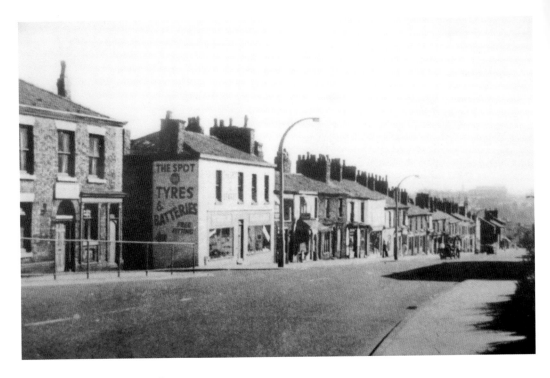

**Lancashire Hill, *c.* 1960 and 2013**

The area around Lancashire Hill has been the site for much industry throughout its time. William Nelstrop founded Nelstrops Millers in 1820 on the site where the mill still stands today. Thomas Rivett and his son, Joseph, established other mills in the area between 1887 and 1897. A 180-foot-tall octagonal brick chimney, belonging to the mills, was felled by the late Fred Dibnah on 2 April 1989. A high-rise residential area now occupies most of the hill site.

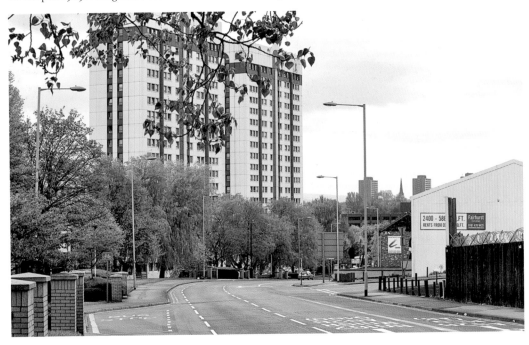

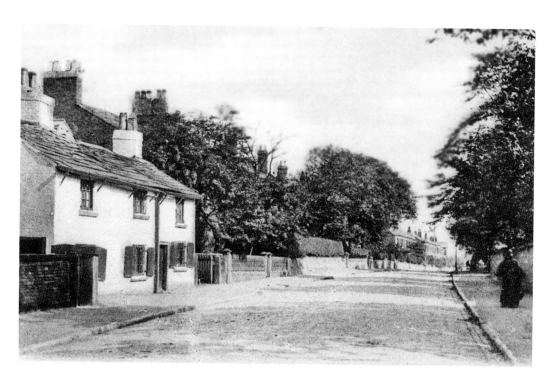

### Manchester Road, 1906 and 2013

Manchester Road is now a busy thoroughfare through Heaton Chapel, and was originally the main route leading from Stockport to Manchester. The original road toll that was collected here should have limited the amount of traffic using it, but the centre of Stockport was congested even during the early 1800s. The new photograph was taken on a quieter Sunday and shows an area still primarily used for private housing and local shops.

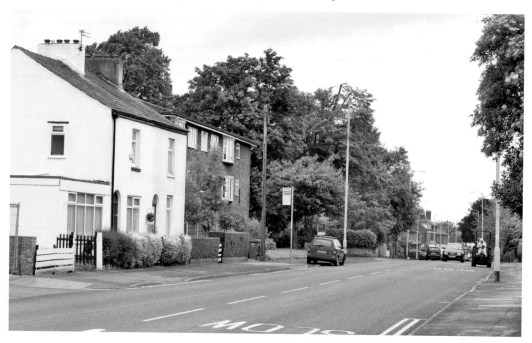

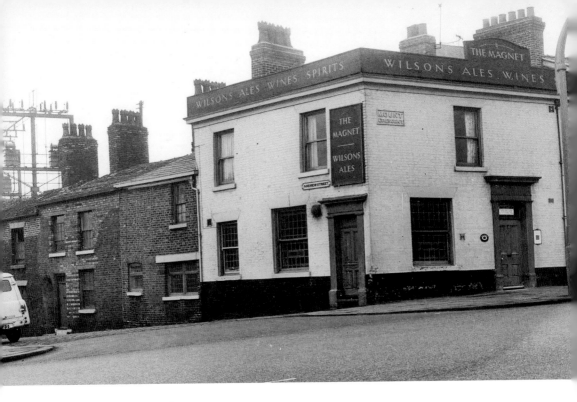

**The Magnet, *c.* 1960 and 2013**

The Magnet public house started out as a coaching inn to help serve the local station of Heaton Norris. It was built in 1840, and the name has been maintained for over 170 years. It is now a popular, award-winning, real ale pub, which serves many cask ales from microbreweries and bottled beers from abroad.

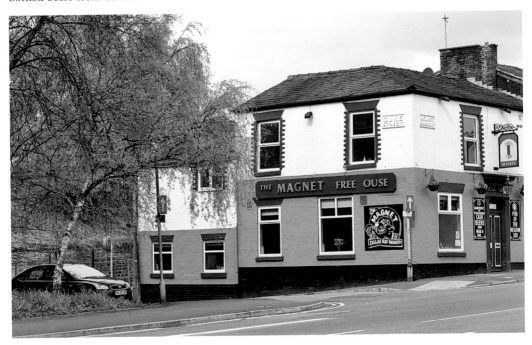

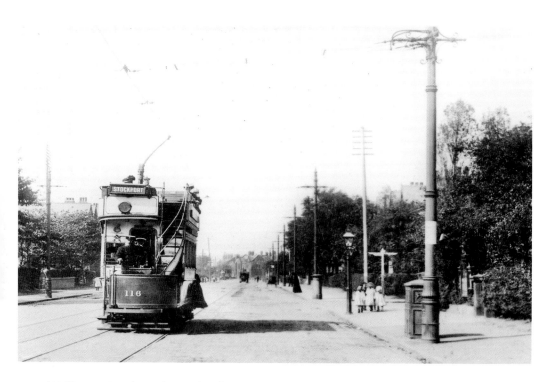

**Wellington Road North, 1906 and 2013**

The popular 192 bus route runs through Heaton Chapel and on to Piccadilly, Manchester. Horse-drawn trams were used from 1889 when the service started at Torkington Road in Hazel Grove. The line was electrified around 1905, and by 1911 was extended to Hazel Grove, though still without a through service to Manchester. The route was first numbered 35 when the full route to Manchester commenced. In 1948, it was renumbered to 92, and then to 192 in 1968 following a reorganisation.

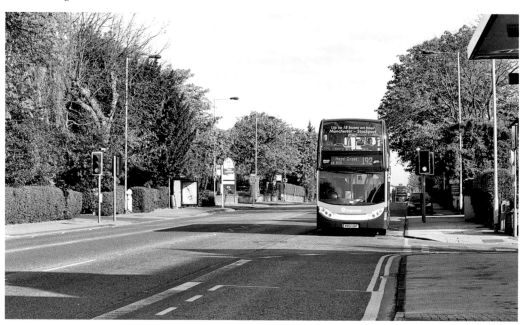

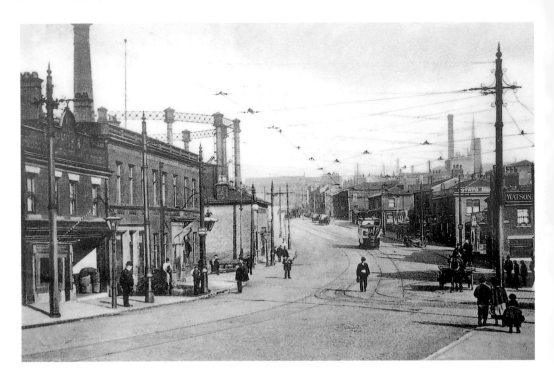

## Wellington Road North, 1905 and 2013

The River Mersey housed many large brick-built factories, making Stockport a major centre of textile manufacture, with cotton spinning and hat making being at the forefront of this industry. Consequently, the landscape looking south towards Stockport town centre has changed drastically since 1905, with many of the mill chimneys disappearing, along with the electric tram wires and the gasworks.

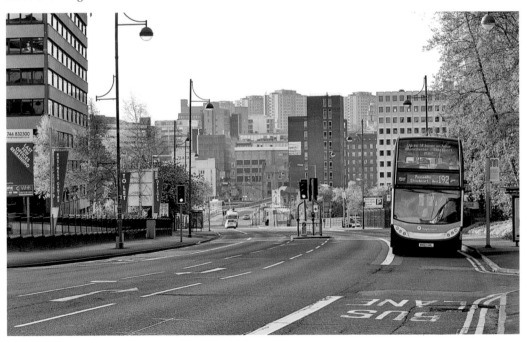

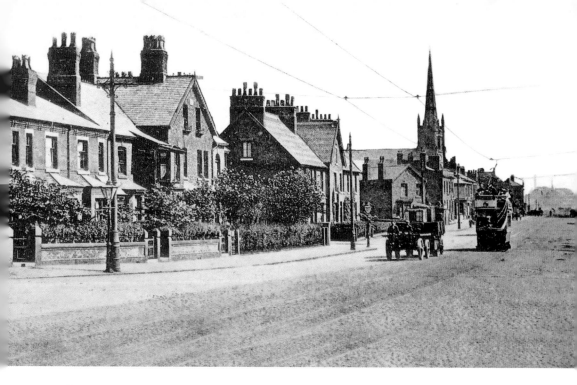

**Wellington Road North, 1909 and 2013**
Church spires and mill chimneys dominated the skyline and acted as landmarks during the 1900s in the Heatons, but today only the church spires remain. Christ church was founded in 1844 and has had a rather chequered history since then. In 1977 it was badly damaged by a fire. However, it has remained a significant feature on Wellington Road over the years and has Grade II listed building status with English Heritage.

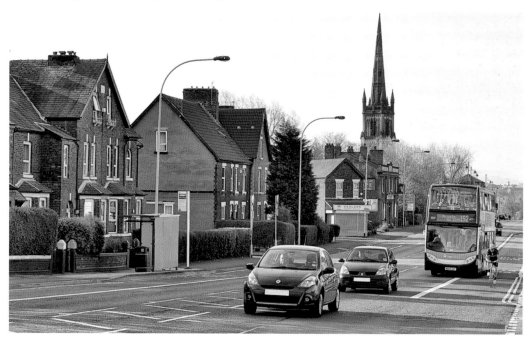

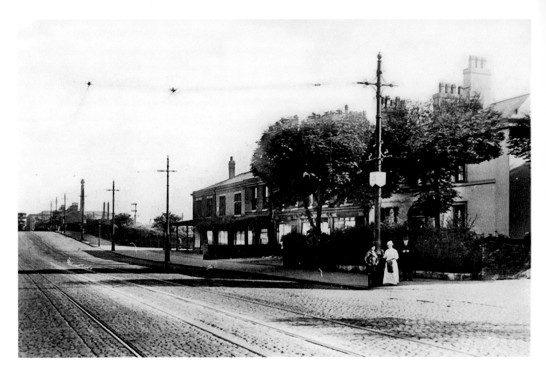

**Wellington Road North, 1915 and 2013**

Wellington Road was constructed after the Napoleonic Wars, and opened with great ceremony in 1826. A tramway serviced Manchester from the early 1900s. It remained in good order throughout; so much so, that the Levenshulme and Stockport section was renewed as late as 1946. The trams were eventually replaced with buses in January 1949. Wellington Road is now the main arterial route through Stockport.

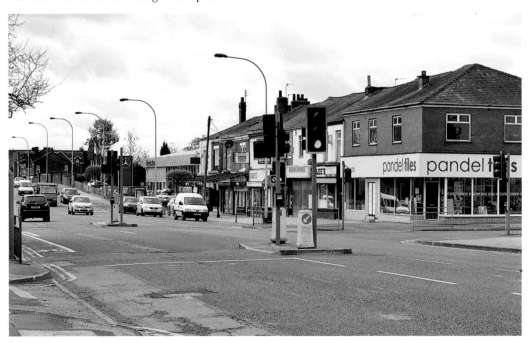

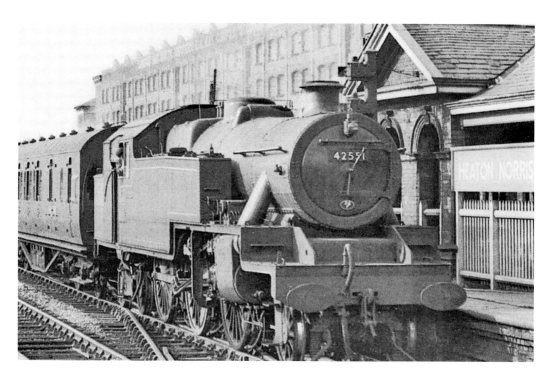

### Heaton Norris Station, 1959 and 2013

The first section of the Manchester and Birmingham Railway was built in 1840 and ran from Manchester to Heaton Norris, where a station was built. The Stockport Viaduct, with its twenty-two arches, was built in 1842 in order to link Heaton Norris with Edgeley, and hence carry the railway over the River Mersey valley. The Heaton Norris station was demoted to a local station when Edgeley station was built in 1843. The station, now demolished, was situated near the far end of the London and North Western Company's Goods Warehouse.

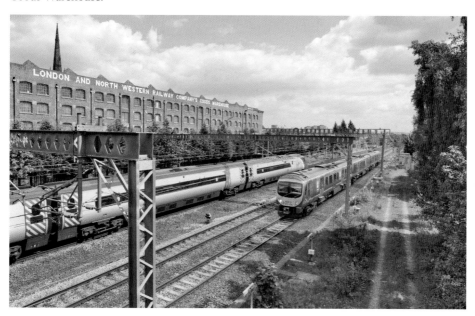

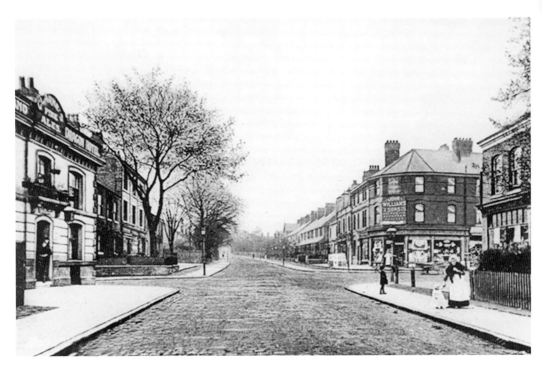

**Manchester Road, 1910 and 2013**

Originally the main route from Stockport to Manchester, Manchester Road ran through Heaton Chapel, forming an important junction with School Lane and Broadstone Road. A toll gate was built opposite St Thomas's church when the road became a turnpike in the early 1720s, but all vehicles had free access after 1873. The road, allegedly the route of a Roman road, carried on and entered Stockport down Lancashire Hill.

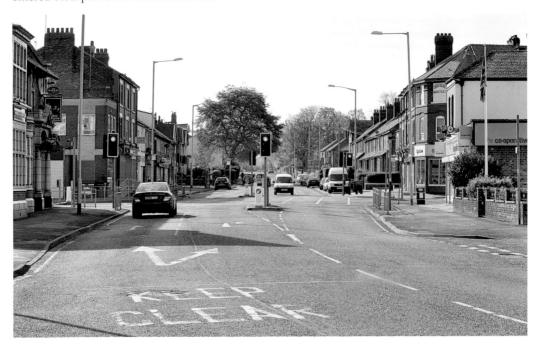

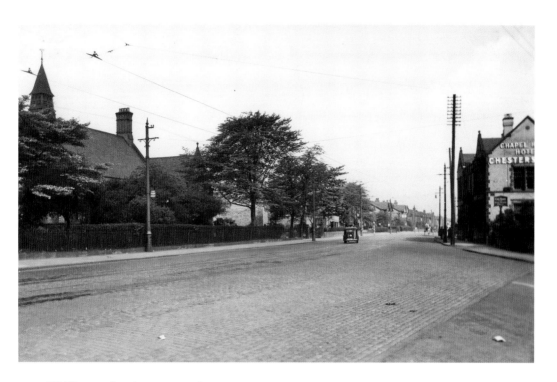

### Wellington Road, *c.* 1930 and 2013

At this junction with Manchester Road, the buildings themselves have changed very little. A Belisha beacon marks a crossing point just ahead of the car, having been introduced to British roads a few years before under the direction of Leslie Hore-Belisha, the Minister for Transport. St Thomas' church and the Chapel House Hotel have retained their character, but sadly the once proud pub is now a Tesco Express.

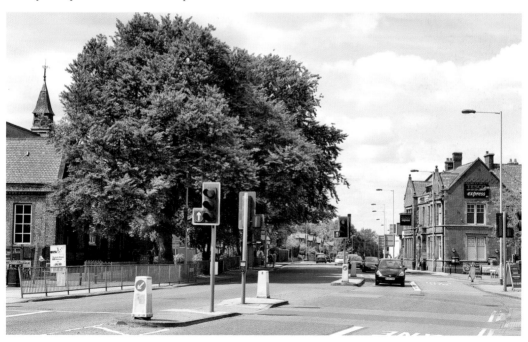

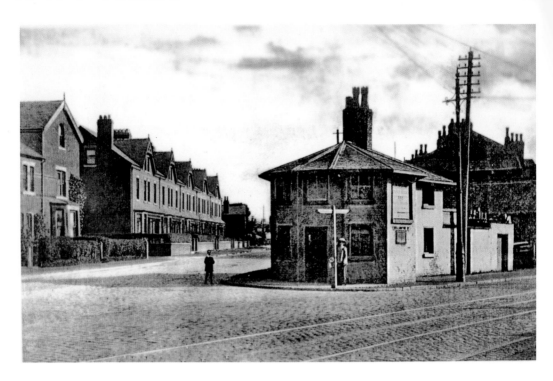

**The Toll Bar, 1910 and 2013**

Acts of Parliament during the eighteenth and nineteenth centuries set up Turnpike Trusts. The trusts collected road tolls for the maintenance of the highway. Manchester Road was the main toll road into Stockport before Wellington Road was built. The toll house at the junction of Manchester Road and Wellington Road North was demolished in a road traffic accident in the 1960s, and has now been replaced by a car showroom.

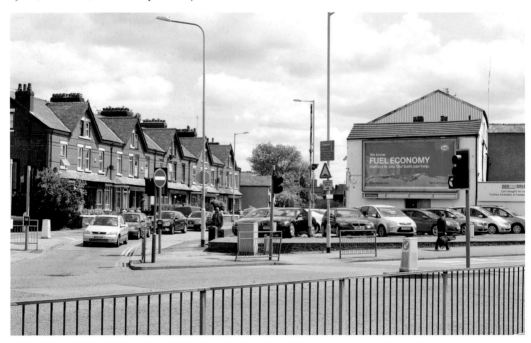

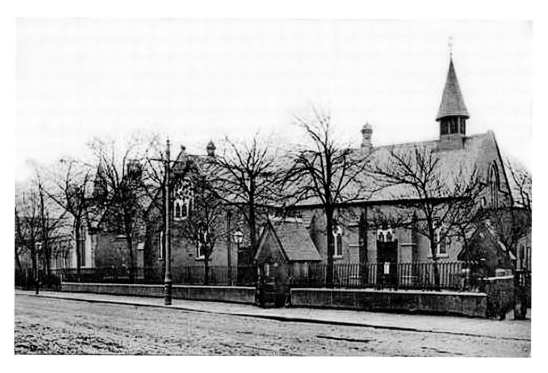

**St Thomas' Church, Wellington Road North, 1909 and 2013**
St Thomas' church was built in 1755. Before it was consecrated in 1765, the building was used as a chapel of ease, giving its name to the area of Heaton Chapel. It was the first place of worship in the Heatons, and, previously, congregations had been expected to walk to chapels in Manchester or Stockport.

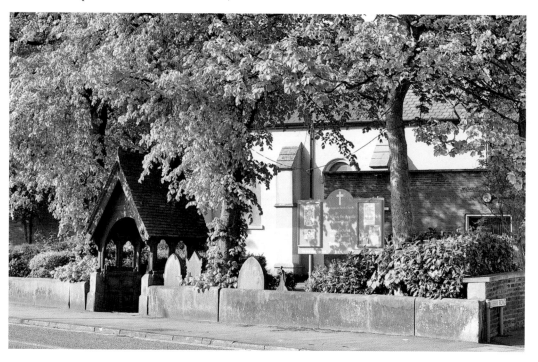

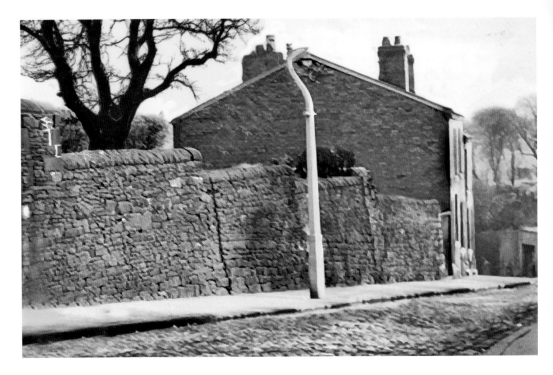

## Dodge Hill, 1970 and 2013

The road, originally called Old Road, formed part of the major north to south route for stagecoaches through Stockport before the Lancashire Hill turnpike road was built in 1794. Much of the road is still a cobbled carriageway, and enhances the nature of this attractive area. The road and area are associated with the Dodge family, who lived nearby before moving to America, where their name is linked to Dodge City and Dodge City Automobiles.

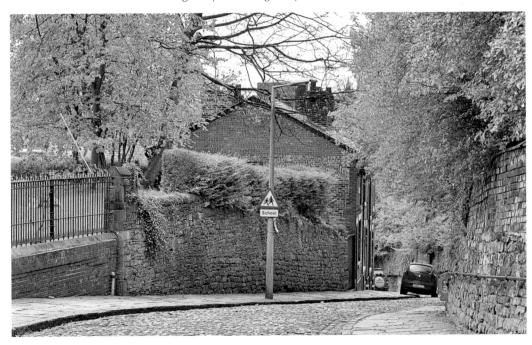

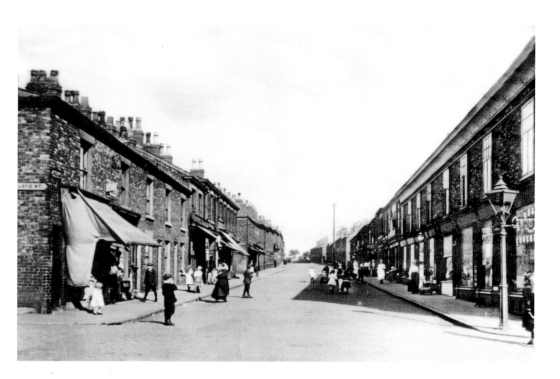

**Love Lane, 1918 and 2013**

The area around Love Lane in 1861 was, by all accounts, a grim place to live and work, due to the closeness of the properties and the pollution from the many mills. The area came to the notice of the nation following the murder of a young child at that time. Today, its cotton manufacturing association has been replaced by private residences and a number of smaller industries.

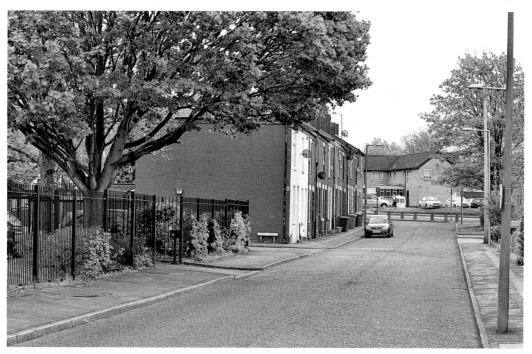

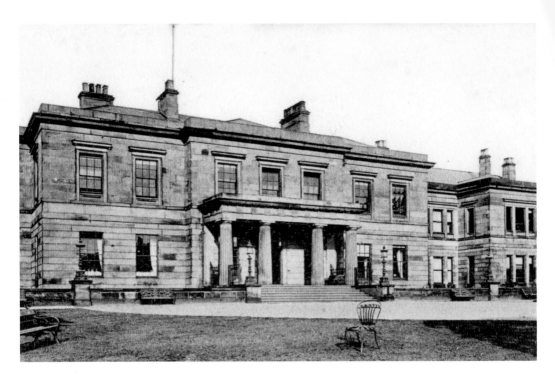

**Mauldeth Hall, 1903 and 2013**

Mauldeth Hall, initially called Leegate Hall, is a large late Grecian villa standing on the edge of the Heatons and Heaton Moor Golf Course. It was built as a family home during the 1830s by the American-born Joseph Cheesborough Dyer. The hall had a number of owners until it became a hospital for incurable diseases in 1880 and, in 1948, an old people's home. It is now the Manchester Chinese Consulate and a Grade II listed building.

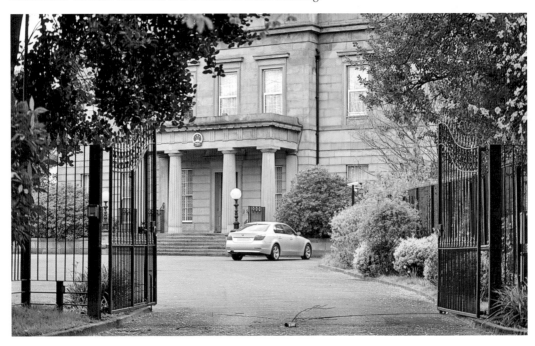

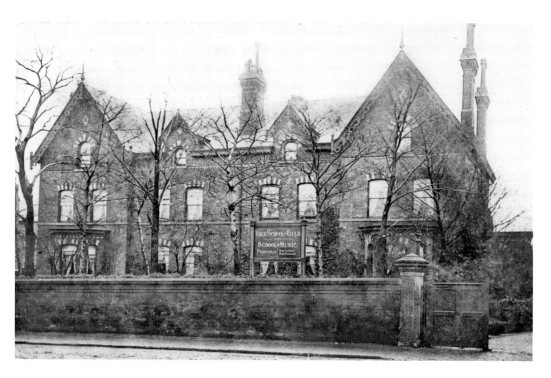

**School of Music, 1904 and 2013**

The High School for Girls and School of Music was situated on Heaton Moor Road opposite Heaton Chapel station, a site that made the school very accessible. The imposing Victorian building now houses a number of apartments, with many of them still retaining their period feel while offering contemporary accommodation.

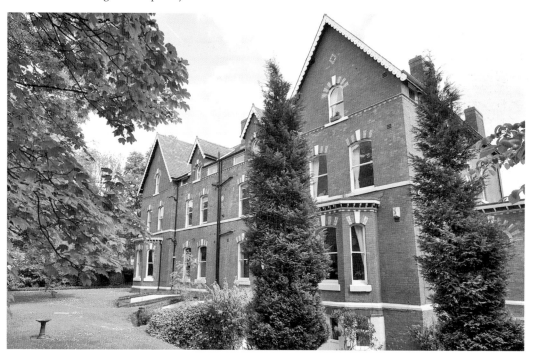

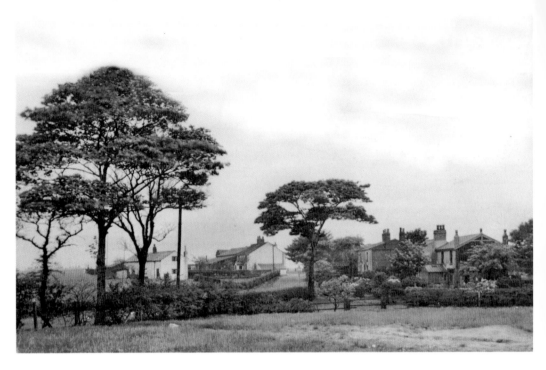

### The Area Near Nelstrop Road, 1908 and 2013

Victorian housing was being developed along Wellington Road and Manchester Road during the late 1800s and early 1900s. Much of the land near where Black Brook runs today was still open farmland, and consequently developed later. New housing complexes have been built since then, but some of the land is still being used as allotments by local residents.

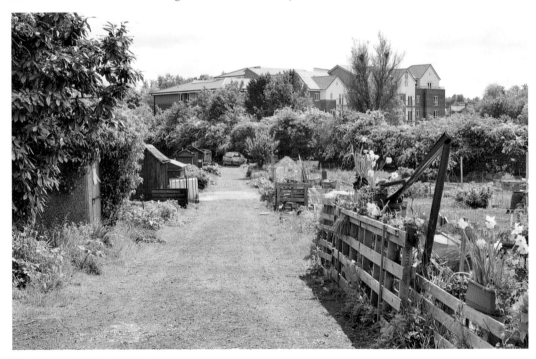

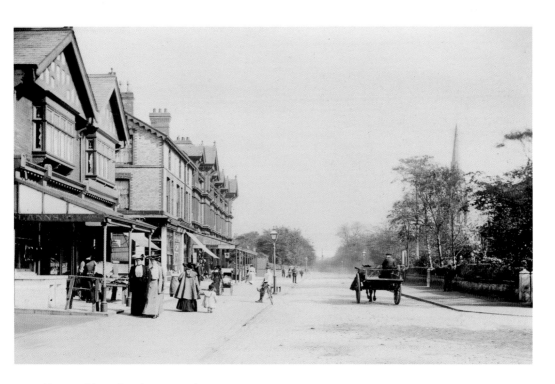

**Heaton Moor Road, 1907 and 2013**

The area along Heaton Moor Road has changed very little since 1907, with the shops on the east side and private residences on the west side of the road. This parade of shops has always provided for local shoppers. Over time, there has been a good range of businesses including a circulating library, Thomas Blagg's ironmongery, chemists, greengrocers and newsagents. Many of the shopfronts and houses still maintain their distinctive Victorian appearance.

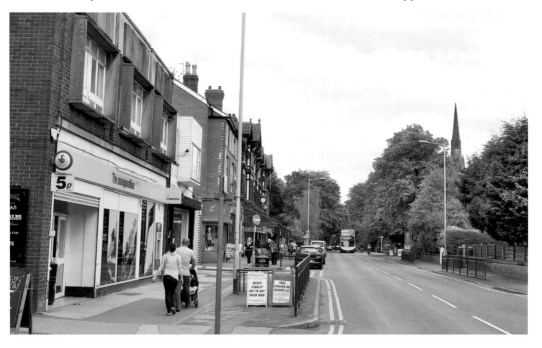

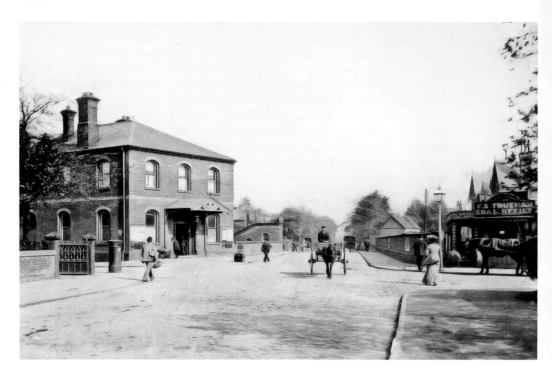

## Heaton Chapel Station, 1917 and 2013

Heaton Chapel station was built in 1852 upon the instigation and influence of a local clergyman, Edward Jackson. The railway station had a great effect on the area because many Manchester businessmen and their families could now live in a leafy suburb and commute to work by train. The same is still true today, and the Friends of Heaton Chapel Station group was formed in 2011 to improve the station by looking after the gardens and mounting art projects.

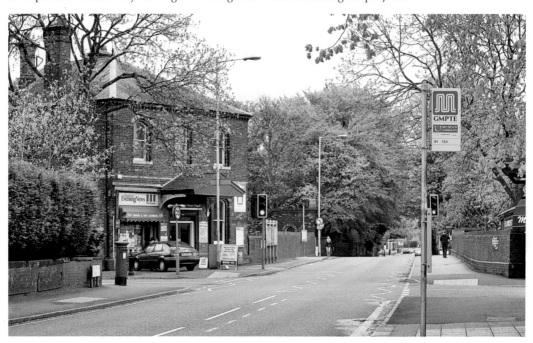